The WIVES' Book

The WIVES' Book

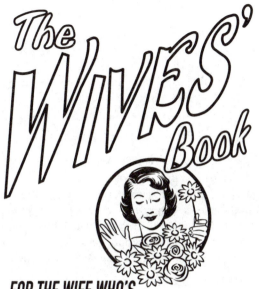

FOR THE WIFE WHO'S

Best AT Everything

ALISON MALONEY

MICHAEL O'MARA BOOKS LIMITED

First published in Great Britain in 2008 by
Michael O'Mara Books Limited
9 Lion Yard, Tremadoc Road
London SW4 7NQ

A CIP catalogue record for this book is available
from the British Library

Papers used by Michael O'Mara Books Limited are
natural, recyclable products made from wood grown in
sustainable forests. The manufacturing processes conform
to the environmental regulations of the country of origin.

ISBN 978-1-84317-325-0

3 5 7 9 10 8 6 4 2

Cover image © David Woodroffe 2008

Illustrations © Robyn Neild 2008

Cover design by Ana Bjezancevic
from an original design by www.blacksheep-uk.com

Designed and typeset by Martin Bristow

Printed and bound in Great Britain by Clays Ltd, St Ives plc

*To Jim, the husband who is best
at everything.*

Contents

CONTENTS

Introduction

Marriage is a wonderful institution, and a cause for celebration, but it isn't always a bed of roses, even for the wife who's best at everything.

Today's time constraints mean that you're usually doing at least three things at once – cooking dinner while tidying the house and bathing the kids, or catching up on paperwork in between answering emails and decorating the spare room. No wonder wives are the most accomplished multi-taskers in the business!

Amid the rush of modern life and the logistics of everyday living, it's great to know that, as a wife, you have someone who is right there beside you for the journey.

This book is a celebration of wives, in all their aspects. As well as practical advice on easy dinners and domestic shortcuts, there are ways to ensure your marriage stays on track, great stories from famous, and not-so-famous, wives, what not to do at the works do, and tips on dealing with the dreaded in-laws.

Most of all, it's a celebration of you, because the wife who's best at everything is a woman of many parts – friend, lover, wage-earner, business partner, companion, domestic goddess, mother and grandmother.

So take some time out and dive into this collection of uxorial gems, because you really are the wife who's best at everything.

The Modern Wife

Today's women quite rightly take it for granted that they can have a successful career as well as marriage and children, if they want, but it isn't that long ago that things were very different indeed.

As recently as the 1930s, women who had jobs were expected to give them up as soon as they married and not just after they had children. And for married women in the earlier part of the century, or at least those without servants, domestic work was a full-time job.

With no vacuum cleaners and dishwashers, cleaning took up a huge amount of time. Washing was done by hand with bars of soap, then wrung through a mangle before being hung out to dry, so the whole of Monday was given over to washing. Many homes had a wash-house, with a brick boiler heated by a fire underneath, and water had to be carried in huge buckets to fill the container.

In a series of memoirs collected by the Ironbridge Museum in Shropshire, an account of a washday at the turn of the century reads:

> On one day in the week, the housewife would gather all the soiled apparel and put them to soak for a time. Then came dollying tubs of hot water, followed by rubbing and wringing, which was severe wrist work, pegging on a clothes line if the weather permitted, and when dry there was folding and placing in a large clothes basket ready to take to the mangle . . . [which] made them beautiful and smooth. After mangling, the housewife would have collars, fronts and cuffs to starch, handkerchiefs etc. to iron. Drying was a problem on wet days.

Even the domestic fridge and freezer are relatively new inventions, so fresh ingredients had to be bought on a daily basis and meals were always cooked from scratch.

As the twentieth century progressed, the invention of domestic appliances, such as the washing machine, tumble dryer and the microwave oven, made life a lot easier for the average housewife. The Second World War, however, had an even greater effect on her life as the absence of men made it necessary for women to work, in some cases for the first time. While women had worked before the war, it was usually only in jobs deemed 'suitable', such as nursing or as a shop assistant. Now they became mechanics, drivers and factory workers. By 1943, almost 90 per cent of single women and 80 per cent of married women were working in factories, on the land or in the armed forces.

The 1960s saw the introduction of the contraceptive pill, which forced its own revolution in and outside of the workplace, since for the first time women could put off having children for the sake of their careers. Legislation in the 1970s gave women equal rights at work so that they were finally able to forge ahead in careers that had been seen as male domains for centuries. Britain even voted in Margaret Thatcher as its first female Prime Minister in 1979.

With women now occupying every walk of life, from doctors lawyers and politicians to electricians and plumbers, it's hard to believe that our grandmothers and great grandmothers spent their married lives chained to a stove and working their socks off to keep the house clean.

As the modern wife juggles work, kids and housework, she can also rely on the best invention of all: the modern husband. Let's face it, life would be a lot harder if he didn't do his share!

THE MODERN WIFE HAS SWAPPED . . .

     ❋ Oven gloves for manicures

   ❋ A shopping basket for a briefcase

    ❋ Baking days for pamper days

      ❋ Sewing for shopping

     ❋ Laundry for lunch

TIPS FOR THE MODERN WIFE

1 If the shoe fits, buy one in every colour.

2 Take life with a pinch of salt – plus a wedge of lime and a shot of tequila.

3 Don't join a support group, have lunch with the girls.

4 Tell him it's PMS – even if you're just being a grumpy cow.

5 If he asks you what you want for your birthday, tell him a card will do – as long as it's a credit card.

6 If he asks where his dinner is, tell him it's at the lovely Italian restaurant round the corner.

7 Don't get your knickers in a twist – it will only make you walk funny.

8 Don't worry about putting on weight – wear higher heels.

9 If you're feeling down, the only way is up.

10 When life gives you lemons, turn them into lemonade, then mix it with vodka.

'I think men who have a pierced ear are better prepared for marriage. They've experienced pain and bought jewellery.'

RITA RUDNER, COMEDIENNE

THE INVENTIONS THAT CHANGED OUR LIVES

1901: H. Cecil Booth patented the vacuum cleaner, but as it was powered by an engine and mounted on a horse-drawn carriage, it wasn't exactly useful to the average housewife.

1903: Earl Richardson of Ontario, California, introduced the lightweight electric iron. Initial reports commented that it overheated in the middle and was cold at the tip, so Richardson made a model with more heat in the point. Everyone wanted the 'iron with the hot point', and in 1905 Hotpoint became his trademark.

1907: Ohio janitor James Spangler came up with the first practical domestic vacuum cleaner, the 'electric suction-sweeper'. It was built from a broom handle, an electric fan and a pillowcase, to hold the dust. The following year he sold the rights to his machine to a relative, one William Hoover.

1908: The Hurley Machine Company of Chicago, Illinois introduced the first electric washing machine, The Thor, invented by Alva J. Fisher. A patent was issued in 1910.

'That quiet mutual gaze of a trusting husband and wife is like the first moment of rest or refuge from a great weariness or a great danger.'

FROM *Silas Marner* BY GEORGE ELIOT

1913: Fred W. Wolf came up with the first domestic refrigerator, a small compartment above an icebox, which needed outside plumbing.

1922: Arthur Leslie Large from Birmingham, England invented the electric kettle.

1937: Bendix Home Appliances introduced the first automatic washing machine.

1945: Percy Spencer discovered the cooking properties of the microwave after noticing that a chocolate bar in his pocket melted while he was working with a radar set. He tried cooking popcorn, then an egg, which exploded. Eventually he fed the electromagnetic field into a metal box and blasted food with microwaves inside. The microwave oven was born.

1949: Marion Donovan from Indiana invented the disposable nappy, but her invention was turned down by established diaper companies so she decided to form her own. After selling her product to Saks in Fifth Avenue, New York, the product proved an instant hit. She sold the patent shortly afterwards for $1 million.

1963: General Electric introduced the self-cleaning oven.

1997: Electrolux came up with the first prototype of a robotic vacuum cleaner. The device works out the room's dimensions and the position of furniture before setting off in a zigzag pattern and turning itself off as soon as it's finished. Clearly the household gadget of the future. Now all we need is a robot that cooks, irons and brings you a cup of tea in bed!

Vintage Advice

'A woman asking "Am I good? Am I satisfied?"
is extremely selfish. The less women fuss about
themselves, the less they talk to other women,
the more they try to please their husbands,
the happier the marriage is going to be.'

DAME BARBARA CARTLAND

Looking back on the advice of yesteryear gives a fascinating
insight into the everyday lives of married women. Even fifty or
sixty years ago, much of the guidance given focused on the
needs of the husband, putting the wife's 'petty troubles' firmly
down the list of priorities. Here are a few pearls of wisdom from
times gone by:

Ten Commandments for Wives

1. Don't bother your husband with petty troubles and
   complaints when he comes home from work.

2. Be a good listener. Let him tell you his troubles; yours
   will seem trivial in comparison.

3. Remember your most important job is to build up and
   maintain his ego (which gets bruised plenty in business).
   Morale is a woman's business.

4. Let him relax before dinner and discuss family problems after the 'inner man' has been satisfied.

5. Always remember he's a male and marital relations promote harmony. Have sane views about sex.

6. No man likes a wife who is always tired out. Conserve your energy so you can give him the companionship he craves.

7. Never hold up your husband to ridicule in the presence of others. If you must criticize, do so privately and without anger.

8. Remember a man is only a grown-up boy. He needs mothering and enjoys it if it isn't piled on too thick.

9. Don't live beyond your means or add to your husband's financial burdens.

10. Don't try to boss him around. Let him think he wears the pants.

Ten Commandments for Husbands

1. Remember your wife wants to be treated as your sweetheart always.

2. Remember her birthdays and your wedding anniversaries.

3. Bring her some gift every week, no matter how inexpensive it may be (it's not the price, it's the thought that counts).

4. Don't take love for granted or 'ration' your kisses. Being a woman, she wants you to woo her.

5. Respect her privacy.

6. Always be tender, kind and considerate, even under trying circumstances.

7. Don't be stingy with money. Be a generous provider.

8. Compliment her new dress, 'hair-do', cooking, etc.

9. Always greet her with a kiss, especially when other people are around.

10. Remember marriage is a 50-50 proposition and you are not the majority stock holder.

From *Sex Today in Wedded Life* by Edward Podolsky, 1947

An intelligent and solicitous wife can mean the difference between the success and the failure of her husband in his career. She will know how to keep an eye on his personal appearance, his wardrobe, and bearing. She will manifest real pride in his undertakings. She will give him generous encouragement, when he is low in spirits, as well as when he is walking on top of the world. She will know how to merit and elicit his confidence, with the assurance that she can be trusted to hold her tongue and to give sound counsel, not that type of silly or emotional reaction which makes a man regret having opened his mouth.

From *The Art of Happy Marriage* by James A. Magner, 1947

- Don't vegetate as you grow older if you happen to live in the country. Some women are like cows, but there is really no need to stagnate. Keep both brain and body on the move.

- Remember it takes two to make a quarrel – don't you be one of them.

- Don't expect your husband to make you happy while you are simply a passive agent. Do your best to make him happy and you will find happiness yourself.

- Don't be out if you can help it when your husband gets home after his day's work.

- Don't let him have to search the house for you. Listen for his latchkey and meet him on the threshold.

From *Don'ts for Wives* by Blanche Ebbutt, 1913

RATE YOUR MARRIAGE

In the 1930s, American psychologist Dr George Crane devised the Marital Ratings Scale, whereby wealthy men could rate the sexual and social merits of their wives by awarding plus or minus points for their behaviour.

A wife who was 'slow to get into bed' or who would 'flirt with other men at parties' was docked points, while she could earn extra points for being a good hostess, keeping a tidy house or putting the children to bed 'personally'.

A wife who used 'slang or profanity' was docked five points, and going to bed in curlers was a serious misdemeanour. Worse was the spouse who put 'cold feet on [her] husband at night to warm them'.

Even their sexual conduct was rated, with a deduction of ten points should she fail to be enthusiastic during 'marital congress' and a bonus of ten points if she reacted to every night of passion with 'pleasure and delight'.

MRS BEETON

Londoner Isabella Beeton was the domestic goddess of her era, publishing her housewife's bible, *Mrs Beeton's Book of Household Management,* in 1861 at the age of twenty-five. It became the must-have item on many a Victorian bride's wedding list and offered tips on every aspect of homemaking, from dealing with the servants to baking collared pig's face for breakfast.

'What moved me, in the first instance, to attempt a work like this, was the discomfort and suffering which I had seen brought upon men and women by household mismanagement,' Mrs

Beeton stated in her introduction. 'I have always thought that there is no more fruitful source of family discontent than a housewife's badly cooked dinners and untidy ways.' Here are a few pieces of advice from this most knowledgeable of mistresses:

On waking early:
'Early rising is one of the most essential qualities which enter into good Household Management, as it is not only the parent of health, but of innumerable other advantages. Indeed, when a mistress is an early riser, it is almost certain that her house will be orderly and well-managed.'

On conversation with friends:
'If the mistress be a wife, never let an account of her husband's failings pass her lips.'

On house calls:

'In making a first call, either upon a newly-married couple, or persons newly arrived in the neighbourhood, a lady should leave her husband's card together with her own, at the same time, stating that the profession or business in which he is engaged has prevented him from having the pleasure of paying the visit with her.'

On dining:

'Food that is not well relished cannot be well digested; and the appetite of the over-worked man of business, or statesman, or of any dweller in towns, whose occupations are exciting and exhausting, is jaded and requires stimulation.

It is in serving up food that is at once appetizing and wholesome that the skill of the modern housewife is severely tasked; and she has scarcely a more important duty to fulfil. It is, in fact, her particular vocation, in virtue of which she may be said to hold the health of the family, and of the friends of the family, in her hands from day to day.'

'She who makes her husband and her children happy, who reclaims the one from vice and trains up the other to virtue, is a much greater character than ladies described in romances, whose whole occupation is to murder mankind with shafts from their quiver, or their eyes.'

**FROM *The Vicar of Wakefield*
BY OLIVER GOLDSMITH, 1761**

Sample menus for 'Plain Family Dinners':

SUNDAY   1. Boiled turbot and oyster sauce, potatoes.
2. Roast leg or griskin of pork, apple sauce, broccoli, potatoes.
3. Cabinet pudding, damson tart made with preserved damsons.

MONDAY   1. The remains of turbot warmed in oyster sauce, potatoes.
2. Cold pork, stewed steak.
3. Open jam tart, which should have been made with the pieces of paste left from the damson tart, baked arrowroot pudding.

TUESDAY   1. Boiled neck of mutton, carrots, mashed turnips, suet dumplings and caper sauce. The broth should be served first, and a little rice or pearl barley should be boiled with it along with the meat.
2. Rolled jam pudding.

WEDNESDAY   1. Roast rolled ribs of beef, greens, potatoes and horseradish sauce.
2. Bread-and-butter pudding, cheesecakes.

THURSDAY   1. Vegetable soup (the bones from the ribs of beef should be boiled down with this soup), cold beef, mashed potatoes.
2. Pheasants, gravy, bread sauce.
3. Macaroni.

FRIDAY 1. Fried whitings or soles.
        2. Boiled rabbit and onion sauce, minced
           beef, potatoes.
        3. Currant dumplings.

SATURDAY 1. Rump-steak pudding or pie, greens,
             potatoes.
          2. Baked custard pudding, stewed apples.

From *Mrs Beeton's Book of Household Management*, 1861

Marriage Marvels

Thomas and Elizabeth Morgan hold the record for the oldest married couple. The Welsh pair were both born in 1786 and married in Caerleon on 4 May 1809. They remained married for eighty-one years and 260 days, until Elizabeth's death on 19 January 1891, two days after her 105th birthday. At the time, Thomas was a mere 104 years and 260 days, giving them a joint age of 209 years and 262 days.

Lauren Lubeck Blair and David E. Hough Blair of Tennessee, USA have married each other eighty-three times in twenty years. The devoted couple first wed in 1984 and have since renewed their vows in the US, the UK and the Dutch Antilles. 'We love telling each other we love each other, and looking into each other's eyes and saying our vows,' explains devoted David.

The longest marriage record is shared by two couples, each married for eighty-six years. Cousins Sir Temulji Bhicaji Nariman and Lady Nariman from India cheated slightly as they were married when they were just five years old in 1853. Their marriage lasted eighty-six years, until Sir Temulji died aged ninety-one years and eleven months in 1940. Lazarus Rowe and Molly Weber were married in Greenland, New Hampshire in 1743 and remained married until Molly's death in 1829.

The oldest couple to wed were Francois Fernandez, ninety-six, and Madeleine Francineau, ninety-four, who got hitched in France in 2002.

The youngest couple ever to get married lived in Aminpur, Bangladesh in 1986, when it was reported that an eleven-month-old boy had been married to a three-month-old girl. The marriage had been arranged in order to end a twenty-year feud between two families.

The world's largest wedding cake was made in Connecticut and weighed 6,818.5 kgs.

Ancient Egyptians believed the vein of love ran from the third finger of the left hand. It is thought that this is where the tradition of wearing the wedding ring on that particular finger originated.

The smallest married couple (in stature) is Douglas Maistre da Silva and Claudia Pereira Rocha. The couple married in Curitiba, Brazil on 26 October 1998. Douglas was 90 cm tall and his bride was slightly taller at 93 cm, making their combined height a mere 1.83 m.

The largest ever mass wedding was held on 25 August 1995, in the Olympic Stadium in Seoul, South Korea, where 35,000 people were married in a ceremony conducted by Sun Myung Moon. Another 325,000 couples around the world participated in the event via satellite link.

In Canada, 85 per cent of brides receive a diamond engagement ring, the highest rate of diamond engagement ring acquisition in the world.

The longest wedding dress train measured 1,362 m and was created by Andreas Evstratiou of bridal shop Green Leaf in Paphos, Cyprus, on 18 February 2007.

There was no expense spared when Mohammed, son of Sheikh Rashid bin Saeed Al Maktoum, wed Princess Salama in 1981. The seven-day celebration in Dubai was the most expensive wedding ever, with a price tag of $44 million (£22 million).

Antigua and Barbuda has the highest marriage rate in the world with 21 marriages per 1000 people per year. The Maldives is next with 20.1.

Which Wife Are You?

As independent as we are, there are certain traits in all of us that conform to type. Below is a rough guide to 'wifestyle', which begs the question, 'Which wife are you?'

THE HIGH-MAINTENANCE MISSUS

This hard-to-please lady may share some traits with the shopaholic (opposite), but it will take more than mere purchases to keep her happy. She wants the lot: money, time, devotion and constant reassurance that she is wonderful. She spends a lot of time making sure she looks perfect and she expects the best in every area of her life. And, boy, will she kick up a stink if she doesn't get it!

MOST LIKELY TO WORK AS: a beautician.

MOST LIKELY TO MARRY: a male model, footballer or the son of an oil tycoon.

MOST LIKELY TO SAY: 'Are you sure I look OK?'

SHE WILL NEVER SAY: 'We'll just make do.'

HE'D BETTER NOT SAY: 'I know your meal's not great, but I don't like to complain.'

THE SHOPAHOLIC

Retail therapy is the name of the game. Let loose with a credit card she will complete the circuit of a shopping centre quicker than a contestant on *Supermarket Sweep*, and money is no object – even when it is.

MOST LIKELY TO WORK AS: a city broker or fashion buyer.

MOST LIKELY TO MARRY: a city broker, barrister or minor royalty.

MOST LIKELY TO SAY: 'There's a sale on at the shopping centre.'

SHE WILL NEVER SAY: 'I think we need to cut back a bit.'

HE'D BETTER NOT SAY: 'Are you *sure* you have nothing to wear?'

THE NURTURER

Caring, kind and loving, this wife will make a perfect mother. Before she hears the patter of tiny feet, however, she will mother her husband instead. She'll be there with his favourite meal, and a smile, when he's had a bad day, and will happily rally round while he puts his feet up. If he's ill, she'll be in her element, providing a constant stream of chicken soup and hot toddies. No matter how exhausted, she'll always have time to cuddle and comfort her fella.

MOST LIKELY TO WORK AS: a doctor, nurse or carer.

MOST LIKELY TO MARRY: anyone who still needs a mother.

MOST LIKELY TO SAY: 'Are you all right?'

SHE WILL NEVER SAY: 'Get over it!'

HE'D BETTER NOT SAY: 'You remind me of my mum.'

THE ICE QUEEN

Always perfectly coiffed, with long, perfectly painted nails, the Ice Queen has one strict rule: look but don't touch. The man she marries may get the occasional cuddle, but only on her terms, and a regular show of affection is not on the cards. Air kisses are more her style than hugs.

MOST LIKELY TO WORK AS: a model or fashion designer.

MOST LIKELY TO MARRY: a travelling salesman or overseas worker.

MOST LIKELY TO SAY: 'Don't touch me; I've just done my nails.'

SHE WILL NEVER SAY: 'Come here and give me a big cuddle.'

HE'D BETTER NOT SAY: 'Go on, let your hair down.'

THE LADETTE

Anything he can do, she can do with him. At the football match, she's hurling so much abuse she'd make a docker blush. If he's going down the pub with his mates, she'll be there with her pint glass at the ready. She may be cramping his style, but she's convinced his pals don't mind her being 'one of the boys'.

MOST LIKELY TO WORK AS: a mechanic or a Radio One DJ.

MOST LIKELY TO MARRY: a rugby player.

MOST LIKELY TO SAY: 'Mine's a pint.'

SHE WILL NEVER SAY: 'I'll have the girls round for a bottle of wine and a chick flick while you're at the pub.'

HE'D BETTER NOT SAY: 'Why don't you ever wear a dress?'

THE FLIRT

Every opportunity to grab some attention from the opposite sex must be seized, whether hubby is around or not. She will do her utmost to look sexy on a night out, accentuating her best assets with low-cut tops, short skirts, or both, and she'll spend the evening talking to every man in the room bar one . . . her husband.

MOST LIKELY TO WORK AS: a receptionist or sales assistant in a menswear shop.

MOST LIKELY TO MARRY: anyone, as long as he doesn't have a jealous streak.

MOST LIKELY TO SAY: 'You're so funny/cute/intelligent!'

SHE WILL NEVER SAY: 'I must go and talk to my husband.'

HE'D BETTER NOT SAY: 'Your skirt's too short.'

THE CAREER GIRL

Ambition is her watchword and woe betide anyone that stands in her way. Her job is her life and her man had better slot in around it. She can't abide slouchers and will only choose a husband who's as ambitious as her.

MOST LIKELY TO WORK AS:
the manager of an international company or self-employed businesswoman.

MOST LIKELY TO MARRY:
the manager of an international company or self-employed businessman.

MOST LIKELY TO SAY:
'I'm working late tonight.'

SHE WILL NEVER SAY:
'It can wait until tomorrow.'

HE'D BETTER NOT SAY:
'It's only a job.'

THE PERFECT HOUSEWIFE

She's an old-fashioned girl at heart and enjoys spending her time cooking and cleaning. Her house is always immaculate and her husband will come home to a perfectly cooked meal every night, served on a pristine tablecloth in a beautiful dining room. The children will be washed and bathed and she will be looking amazing by the time he gets home from work. Think Bree from *Desperate Housewives*!

MOST LIKELY TO WORK AS: a housewife.

MOST LIKELY TO MARRY: a hardworking professional who can ensure she won't need to help out with the mortgage.

MOST LIKELY TO SAY: 'Please take your shoes off before you come in.'

SHE WILL NEVER SAY: 'I can't be bothered to clean the oven.'

HE'D BETTER NOT SAY: 'I'll just leave my muddy boots in the kitchen.'

'Grief can take care of itself, but to get the full value of joy, you must have somebody to divide it with.'

MARK TWAIN

Words of Wisdom

Wedded bliss takes a lot of planning, so start as you mean to go on. In the interest of future harmony there are some things that a wife should never say to her husband. After all, he might think she means them.

Here are a few examples of phrases you may live to regret:

* 'You should go out with your mates more often.'
  (*He will.*)

* 'I don't really need a night out with the girls.'
  (*Yes, you do.*)

* 'If you want a new sports car, we don't *have* to go on holiday this year.'
  (*You'll hate that car.*)

* 'Look at that twenty-year-old. Don't you think she's attractive?'
  (*You really don't want an honest answer to that.*)

* 'Of course I don't want you to cook tonight.'
  (*You may enjoy cooking, but never turn down an offer to hand over the oven gloves. It might be a long time before he asks again.*)

* 'I think flowers are lame.'
  (*Ten years down the line, you'll be lucky if he remembers your anniversary, let alone buys you flowers. Accept them while you can.*)

* 'It's definitely my turn to change the nappy.'
  (*That's one job it's always good to delegate.*)

* 'Don't buy me anything for my birthday.'
  (*He won't.*)

* 'If you can't get the time off work, I'll go to all three nativity plays/sports days.'
  (*You'll definitely live to regret that offer.*)

* 'I can't stand your mother.'
  (*The ultimate marital faux pas.*)

If you're lucky in love, your husband will always come up with the appropriate phrase to make you feel better in any situation. Any of the following, repeated on a regular basis, is bound to make for a happy marriage:

* 'Put your feet up, darling.'

* 'That dress looks amazing.'

* 'I'll do the washing up.'

* 'Yes, that really is a bargain.'

* 'I love you.'

* 'Take *my* credit card.'

* 'Ding dong – Tiffany calling!'

* 'The kids are going to stay with my parents. We're going to Venice for the weekend.'

✳ 'Let's get a takeaway.'

✳ 'You still look as great as the day we met.'

TEN DON'TS FOR HIS OFFICE DO

❶ Practise pole dancing on the dance floor.

❷ Suggest endless ways of making the company and your husband more efficient.

❸ Get horribly drunk and throw up in the dinner.

❹ Tell his work colleagues exactly what he thinks of them.

❺ Challenge the weedy security guard to an arm-wrestling contest – and win.

❻ Bribe the DJ to play nothing but slow numbers and then spend the night smooching with your hubby.

❼ Insist on getting up and singing a song – even though it isn't a karaoke night.

❽ Start a food fight.

❾ Snog the boss.

❿ Snog the boss's wife.

Anniversary Treats

Just because men are notoriously bad at remembering anniversaries doesn't mean you should do the same. Your wedding anniversary is a time to celebrate your marriage all over again, so make it special and push the boat out. If he has forgotten, he'll be so sheepish he'll never forget it again!

A RACY DAY

Treat him to a day driving the car of his dreams. Race tracks and driving schools run gift days where car enthusiasts can experience how it feels to be behind the wheel of a Formula One car, a Ferrari, Lamborghini or rally car. It's a brilliant gift he'll never forget.

ROMANCE REVISITED

Book a table at your favourite restaurant and treat it like a date. Arrange to meet him there rather than arriving together, and make sure you're ten minutes late – or even later if he's a bit lax about punctuality. Spend more time than usual on your hair and make-up, and wear your sexiest outfit so you knock him dead when you walk in. Spend the evening flirting and playing footsie under the table and, for dessert, make sure you're wearing sexy underwear to match the outfit!

HOT AND FLIGHTY

Providing he's not afraid of heights, a trip in a hot-air balloon is the perfect way to spend your anniversary. If you don't fancy it yourself, buy a flight for him for a future date, or make a day of it by going together and having lunch in the country. This is not a budget gift, but it makes a really memorable day out.

FOOTIE FAN

If he's a football fan, you could make his day – and year – by forking out for a season ticket for his favourite club. Not only will he be over the moon, you'll get him out from under your feet every Saturday for months. If that's too expensive (and it may well be) then buy him a tour of his team's stadium. Tour tickets are very reasonable and he'll get a great look at what goes on behind the scenes.

HONEYMOON HEAVEN

Remember how wonderful it felt to be on honeymoon with your new husband? Whether you went to Margate or Marrakesh, there was bound to be romance in the air, so bring a little honeymoon into your home by recreating the food you ate and the décor of your favourite holiday restaurant. If you went to Italy, for example, cook a favourite pasta dish and decorate the table with a checked tablecloth, candles and a bottle of Italian wine. After your romantic meal, bring out the honeymoon photos and reminisce together.

PICNIC PASSION

When was the last time you went for a picnic in the country? If the weather's fine, there's nothing lovelier than a trip to the countryside and an al fresco lunch. Pack a basket or cool bag with bread and cheese, cold meats, pâté and fruit. Take a bottle of wine or a flask of tea and make sure you pack a picnic blanket to sit on. Find a lovely spot in the woods or on a riverbank, and while away the hours eating, chatting and daydreaming.

RENEW YOUR VOWS

What better way to celebrate your marriage than to reaffirm your love for each other? It's a great way to mark a special anniversary, such as a tenth or twenty-fifth, and if you have kids, it's a special occasion for them, too. Ceremonies can be conducted just about anywhere you like, including churches, chapels, hotels, banqueting suites or even the privacy of your own home. Vow renewals are a warm and touching way to say, 'I love you – still,' in front of your family and friends, and they're not half as stressful to arrange as weddings!

RIVER ROMANCE

There's something inescapably romantic about being on the water, so if you live within driving distance of a river, look into the possibility of a riverboat cruise. There is usually something to suit every budget, from a river-bus sightseeing trip to dinner for two on board a luxury yacht.

DANCING CHEEK TO CHEEK

Ballroom and Latin dancing are all the rage at the moment, so buy an anniversary gift you can both enjoy: a dance lesson. Book a one-to-one lesson to find out if you enjoy going to a class together – it might lead to a shared hobby, which is not only great fun, it will keep you fit too. You never know, he might be the next Mark Ramprakash.

'We are told that people stay in love because of chemistry, or because they remain intrigued with each other, because of many kindnesses, because of luck. But part of it has got to be forgiveness and gratefulness.'

ELLEN GOODMAN, US COLUMNIST

THEME IT

Plan your gift or outing to reflect the anniversary you're celebrating. For example, the first anniversary is paper, so buy a book or a writing set. The ninth is pottery or willow, so you could spend the day at a pottery class making your own creations or buy tickets to see the cricket. The fourteenth is ivory, so why not go to a piano bar and watch someone tinkle the ivories for the evening?

WEDDING ANNIVERSARY GIFTS

YEAR	BRITISH	AMERICAN
1st	Paper	Paper
2nd	Cotton	Cotton
3rd	Leather	Leather
4th	Fruit, Flowers	Linen, Silk
5th	Wood	Wood
6th	Sugar	Iron
7th	Wool, Copper	Wool, Copper
8th	Bronze	Bronze
9th	Pottery, Willow	Pottery
10th	Tin	Tin, Aluminium
11th	Steel	Steel
12th	Silk, Linen	Silk
13th	Lace	Lace
14th	Ivory	Ivory
15th	Crystal	Crystal
20th	China	China
25th	Silver	Silver
30th	Pearl	Pearl
35th	Coral	Coral, Jade
40th	Ruby	Ruby
45th	Sapphire	Sapphire
50th	Gold	Gold
55th	Emerald	Emerald
60th	Diamond	Diamond
65th	Star sapphire	Star sapphire
70th	Platinum	Platinum
75th	Diamond	Diamond

Meet the Family

You can choose your man but you can't choose his family. Your perfect fella could come with a whole host of relatives you detest. If you adore your in-laws you are a lucky woman. If not, read the following very carefully.

TEN GOLDEN RULES TO KEEP IN WITH THE IN-LAWS

1 **Never insult his parents**
He may spend half his time complaining about his mum or dad but you have to learn to bite your tongue, even if you agree with him. If you join in the character-assassination, the chances are he'll switch sides and start defending them. Imagine how you would feel if he criticized your parents.

2 **Be on your best behaviour**
Family occasions may be a trial, but don't overcompensate by getting smashed and ending up under the table. Try not to flirt with your husband's favourite uncle and don't do the conga round the lawn and end up face down in his mum's prize lobelias.

3 **Don't try too hard**
Be nice, be charming, but don't overdo it. It's fine to bring flowers or chocolates when they invite you for dinner and

to compliment the meal they serve, but don't make the whole conversation about how wonderful the house/the garden/the meal/her dress is.

4 **Be tactful**

If your husband has told you secrets about his mum and dad, or even just told you his mum's cooking is atrocious, there's never any need for them to know. When the dessert goes wrong and tastes disgusting, force it down anyway and tell them it's fine.

5 **Respect her right to be Mum**

Mummy's little boy is always going to be special to her so you won't find your way into her heart by constantly picking fault with him. Equally, if she is a possessive type don't drape yourself all over him every time you meet. You may have to go a long way to prove you're good enough for him, so be careful.

6 **Accept their differences**

Your in-laws may not have brought up their children the way your parents did, and may have different values. But nobody's perfect, not even you. And remember that they must have done something right – after all they raised a man you fell in love with. Accept their differences and faults as part of the whole package.

7 **Listen to advice**

Don't dismiss everything they tell you because it seems outdated. Like your own parents, they have more experience of life than you two and have been through the early years of marriage themselves. Listen to them, and even seek their advice occasionally, especially if you have children. They will appreciate that you asked and warm to you more.

8 Be friends – to a point

Your in-laws, including brothers, sisters and parents, can be good friends, if you're lucky. Arrange nights out with his family or ask your mother-in-law or sister-in-law to come when you fancy a day shopping, or going to a girly movie. Don't overdo it, though, if it makes your husband uncomfortable. He may think you spend the whole day talking about him!

9 Avoid family fallouts

If your husband falls out with his parents/sister/brother – keep well away from the row. Don't take sides and *never* intervene. If you put your twopenn'orth in it will only be held against you, probably long after your husband is forgiven.

10 Don't take advantage

If your in-laws are the generous sort and happy to help you out when you need a babysitter, a lift, or a loan, remember the relationship doesn't end there. Make sure they know you enjoy their company even when you don't want a favour. If they've been running around after you recently, cook them a nice meal to say thanks.

Domestic Goddess

Juggling work with kids, hobbies or trips to the gym means there's little time for housework. Let's face it, few of us would put washing floors and dusting at the top of our list of favourite things to do!

But necessity is the mother of invention, and if you want to free up some of your precious time to do the things you actually enjoy, there are plenty of housework shortcuts that mean running the home needn't be a chore. These tips will show you how, with the minimum of work, you can convince your friends and family you truly are a domestic goddess.

DIVIDE AND RULE

A woman's work is never done, so the saying goes, but it's a damn sight easier if the bloke does his share!

Muddling through each day and landing yourself with jobs you hate will only lead to resentment, so sit down and work out a list that suits you both. If he loves cooking, make that one of his jobs as often as possible. If he hates ironing but is happy to push a Hoover round, then he can do that while you iron his shirts. If you both hate cleaning the loo, then take it in turns.

A clear division of labour will mean fewer arguments, but at the same time be realistic. If he gets home from work three hours after you, or vice versa, sharing the daily chores equally is clearly unfair. Work out what needs to be done when, and who has the time to do which jobs.

BE FLEXIBLE

Having written your list and divided the housework, remember to take everyday circumstances into account. Nothing will annoy you more than him putting his feet up and watching the football because he's finished his list, while you're still up to your elbows in soap suds. Equally, if he's promised to Hoover and is still mowing the lawn while you're free, help him out.

JUST LEAVE IT

Perfect housewives often make more work for themselves than necessary and can do more harm than good. Here are a few jobs you really *don't* have to do on a regular basis:

✳ **DRYING UP:** Letting your dishes dry on the draining board not only saves work, it's more hygienic.

✳ **POLISHING FURNITURE:** Most experts believe that wooden furniture should be cleaned with a slightly damp cloth and not polished to within an inch of its life. Too much polishing can damage the wood.

✳ **CUPBOARDS:** The insides of most wardrobes, drawers and cupboards don't need regular cleaning, though cupboards used to store food may need the occasional clear-out.

✳ **HOOVERING:** The main thoroughfares of the house will need regular vacuuming – how often will depend on how many people and pets are wandering about. But you don't have to move the sofas and pull all the furniture about every time. Go for a deeper clean once a month or so.

✳ **POLISHING THE SILVER:** Silver should be washed in warm (not hot) soapy water and dried with a clean tea towel. If this is done regularly, polishing is hardly ever necessary.

KEEP IT QUICK

The bathroom

Apart from the living room and kitchen, the bathroom is the one place visitors are likely to go, so if it sparkles at all times, even on unexpected visits, they will be suitably impressed.

The key to keeping a spotless bathroom is daily attention. That doesn't mean scrubbing the sink for half an hour a day – just giving it a daily five-minute once-over will mean no more grimy sinks and grubby bath rings.

* Keep a spray-bottle full of a soda-crystal or mild detergent solution, along with a cloth, somewhere in the bathroom. When you've finished brushing your teeth in the morning, spray the sink and bath taps with the solution and quickly wipe around. That way the soap scum and dirt won't have time to build up.

✱ After using the sink each time, wipe the taps with a bath towel to leave them gleaming.

✱ Keep a 14-in (35-cm) squeegee (as used by window cleaners) hanging in or near the shower and use it to wipe the shower dry before stepping out. It cuts down on a lot of mildew and limescale build-up. Alternatively, use a daily shower spray.

The kitchen
This is where the messiest pursuit in the house takes place – cooking. When it comes to cleaning, there are few things as disheartening as work surfaces encrusted with dried-on food, blobs of tomato sauce up the walls and a cooker caked in baked-on grease, so once again the key is not to leave it.

✱ After each meal, either wash up or load the dishes into the dishwasher.

✱ Wipe surfaces with a spray of detergent or soda-crystal solution. Diluted vinegar can be used on some surfaces, but not on marble or granite.

✱ Most ovens are self-cleaning (hurrah!) which means a build-up of grease on the roof and sides is unlikely. The rest can be cleaned with a paste of bicarbonate of soda, salt and hot water. Leave it on for fifteen minutes, then rinse thoroughly.

✱ Wipe all food spills from the hobs *immediately* using a mild detergent or washing-up liquid. Don't wait until after dinner because it will be twice as hard.

✳ Wipe oven spills up as soon as possible. Splattered grease on the door of the grill or oven should be wiped with a damp cloth and washing-up liquid.

✳ Once in a while remove any grease build-up from walls with a warm solution of soda crystals. One cup in a bucket or washing-up bowl of warm water will do it.

✳ Wash the floor with vinegar solution (one cup) and a few drops of washing-up liquid in a bucket of warm water. A mop with a bucket and built-in wringer make this a much quicker job.

The twenty-minute spruce-up

You've just got through the door and your mother-in-law or house-proud sister rings to say she's popping round for a cuppa. The house is a tip, but don't panic! A quick spruce-up can make all the difference.

✳ **PRIORITIZE**: Which rooms will your visitor actually see? Concentrate on the hallway, living room, kitchen and bathroom – or wherever they're most likely to go – then start with the worst offender.

✳ **CONCEAL**: If you have a dishwasher, bung all your dirty dishes in it. If not, bung them in the oven (just make sure you remember they're there before you turn it on). Then wipe all the kitchen surfaces.

✳ **DECLUTTER**: Pick up clothes, toys, books etc. from the reception rooms, and if you haven't got time to put them away, bung them in a room your visitor won't go in. Alternatively, if your house is often strewn with toys, books and clothes, keep a large wicker basket somewhere on the ground floor so you can chuck them all in it at a moment's notice.

✳ **DETRASH**: If you have children (or a husband) who are in the habit of leaving food wrappers and empty drink cartons lying around, grab a bin bag or cardboard box and do a quick scan of the rooms for offending items.

✳ **SHINE**: Using spray detergent or cream cleanser, wipe the sink and taps in the bathroom and kitchen. Sparkling sinks and gleaming taps create the impression of a clean house.

✳ **MAKE BEDS**: Leave this until last as it's unlikely many visitors will go into the bedrooms. If they will be, make sure the bedclothes are pulled up and straight, and hide any clean washing under the duvet cover if you haven't got time to put it away.

More quick fixes

* To remove limescale from a bath, soak some cloths in vinegar and lay them over the limescale patches before you go to bed. Rinse them in the morning and wipe over with a clean cloth. Your bathroom might smell like a chip shop for a few hours, but your bath will be gleaming.

* If your shower-head looks scummy, put a mixture of half a cup of vinegar and half a cup of baking soda in a strong sandwich bag and tie it around the shower-head for an hour. Remove, wipe the top of the shower-head and turn on the water for a few seconds to rinse.

* To clean tarnished silver, line a washing-up bowl or plastic container with aluminium foil, shiny side up. Then add a cup of warm water and a teaspoon of bicarbonate of soda. Soak the silver items in the solution for a few seconds, rinse and dry.

* Don't worry if your ready-meal has exploded in the microwave and the walls are covered in dried tomato sauce. Place a slice of lemon in a bowl, cover with water and microwave for five minutes, then wipe the insides of the microwave with a damp cloth.

* Clean your dishwasher once a month by placing an upright cup of vinegar in the top basket, then run the empty machine through a normal cycle.

* Wash dirty fingerprints and black marks off walls and paintwork with a cup of soda crystals dissolved in a bucket of warm water.

Queen of Cuisine

Cooking may be fun for some, but thinking up a nutritious, balanced meal every other night can be a drag. The trick is to store up a few recipes that are quick, easy and bound to impress. Pasta dishes and stir fries are brilliant when you're pushed for time, but you can't do them every night, so here are a few recipes that take very little time to prepare – though he'll never guess it!

HUEVOS A LA FLAMENCA

This is a beautiful Spanish dish which isn't too spicy and can be made in about 20–30 minutes. The beauty of this recipe is that it's also delicious without the meat if you're vegetarian. As the meat is the one of the last things to go in, you can set aside a vegetarian portion before adding it.

SERVES 4
450 g/1 lb potatoes, peeled and cubed
1 large onion, chopped
1 tin of chopped tomatoes
1 tin or jar of pimentos (sweet red peppers)
in brine, roughly chopped
½ cup peas
6 slices of pepperoni
or 2 children's pepperoni sticks, chopped
1 thick slice of ham (approx 1 cm thick), cubed
Salt and pepper
4 eggs

1. Preheat the oven to 180°C/350°F/gas mark 4.

2. Parboil the potatoes for 5 minutes, then drain.

3. Fry the onion in a large pan until soft, then add the tomatoes, pimentos and half the brine from the jar.

4. Add the potatoes and peas and bring to the boil.

5. Stir in the meat and season to taste (you won't need much salt with the pepperoni).

6. Place the mixture in a baking dish and break one egg per person on top.

7. Bake in the oven for about 20 minutes, or until the egg whites have set.

TOP TIP: For an even quicker way to cook the eggs, crack the eggs on the top of the mixture while it's still in the saucepan. Make sure you have plenty of liquid in the sauce and add water if necessary. Spoon the hot liquid over the eggs to speed up cooking time and be careful the sauce doesn't burn at the bottom.

EASY CHICKEN CASSEROLE

SERVES 4

6 small or 4 large chicken breasts,
cut into 2.5 cm strips
1 large onion, chopped
100 g/3½ oz button mushrooms, sliced
600 ml/1 pint chicken stock
1 glass red or white wine
1 bouquet garni
Salt and pepper

1 Preheat the oven to 180°C/350°F/gas mark 4.

2 Place the chicken in a large casserole dish together with the onion and mushroom, then add the stock, wine, bouquet garni and seasoning.

3 Cover and cook for approximately one hour, removing the lid for the last 20 minutes to reduce.

TOP TIPS: This is great served with a jacket potato, which can cook in the oven at the same time. Leftovers can be liquidized with some extra stock to make a lovely chicken soup – add crème fraîche or cream to make it richer.

SAUSAGE CASSEROLE

This dish couldn't be easier and it tastes delicious. For a vegetarian version, use Quorn or any meat-free sausages.

SERVES 3–4
8 sausages
450 g/1 lb potatoes, peeled and cubed
1 large onion, sliced
850 ml/1½ pints stock
1 teaspoon dried thyme
Salt and pepper

1 Preheat the oven to 180°C/350°F/gas mark 4.

2 Brown the sausages under the grill, then cut each one into four pieces.

3 Put all the ingredients in a large casserole, season to taste, cover and bake in the oven for about an hour, until the potatoes are cooked.

4 Delicious served with baked beans.

LIPSMACKING LASAGNE

Home-made lasagne is in a totally different class to the ready-meal variety, but many people are put off making it because it looks difficult. It really isn't.

SERVES 4
1 tablespoon olive oil
450 g/1 lb minced lamb or beef
1 large onion, chopped
1 garlic clove, crushed (optional)
100 g/4 oz mushrooms, sliced
1 tin chopped tomatoes
6 tablespoons tomato purée
¼ teaspoon dried basil
Salt and pepper
Approx. 150 g/5½ oz lasagne sheets
40 g/1½ oz cornflour
570 ml/1 pint milk
100 g/4 oz cheddar cheese, grated

❶ Preheat the oven to 200°C/400°F/gas mark 6.

❷ Using a large saucepan or frying pan, fry the onions and garlic in the olive oil on a low heat until soft, then add the mince, turn the heat up and fry for a further few minutes until brown.

❸ Add the mushrooms, tomatoes, tomato purée, basil and seasoning and simmer for 20 minutes.

❹ Next make the cheese sauce by combining a little of the cold milk with the cornflour in a pan to make a wet paste, then add a little more milk and stir thoroughly.

5 Place the pan on the hob, adding milk gradually and stirring or whisking constantly to prevent lumps forming.

6 Bring to the boil, stir in most of the cheese, then remove from the heat. Season to taste.

7 In a large lasagne dish, layer the meat and lasagne sheets, finishing off with a layer of lasagne.

8 Pour the cheese sauce on top of the lasagne, making sure none of the pasta shows.

9 Sprinkle the remaining cheese on top and bake in the oven for 30 minutes, or until the top is golden brown.

10 Serve with a salad.

TOP TIP: If there are only two of you, it's worth making a full-size lasagne because it's easy to reheat or freeze for a later date.

The Art of Leftovers

Around a third of the food we buy is thrown out – much of it when it's still edible – which not only has an impact on the environment but also on our pockets.

Part of the problem is the BOGOF – the buy-one-get-one-free supermarket offer that seems too good to resist – and the fact that we tend to do one big shop a week or even fortnight, which inevitably means we end up with too much in our trolleys.

When our parents and grandparents set up house, there were local shops where they would buy whatever they needed for the next day or two, so there was no need to plan a fortnight's menu in one go.

The other problem is that many of us simply don't know what to do with leftovers, despite the fact that there are hundreds of great recipes that use up leftover meat, fish and vegetables. But before you whip out the casserole dish and last night's chicken, take a look at these basic safety guidelines:

* Refrigerate leftovers within two hours of cooking.

* Don't forget they are there – they should be eaten within four days.

* Only reheat leftovers once. If there's still some food left over after the second heating, throw it away.

BEEF AND ONION STEW

SERVES 4
115 g/4 oz butter
2 large onions, chopped
1 tablespoon flour
1 tablespoon vinegar
1 teaspoon Dijon mustard (optional)
Approx. 600 ml/1 pint beef stock
1 teaspoon dried thyme
Salt and pepper
450 g/1 lb leftover beef, thinly sliced
Breadcrumbs

1 Preheat the oven to 180°C/350°F/gas mark 4.

2 Melt the butter in a large pan and fry the onions until soft.

3 Add the flour, mixing it into the butter, and cook for a further 2 minutes.

4 Stir in the vinegar and mustard, then add enough stock to make a thin sauce.

5 Add the thyme and seasoning and simmer for around 30 minutes.

6 Cover the bottom of a shallow dish with some sauce, then layer beef slices on top. Alternate sauce and meat slices, ending with the sauce.

7 Cover the dish and bake in the oven for an hour, checking occasionally to make sure the sauce doesn't reduce too much – if it does add more stock.

8. Remove from the oven and sprinkle liberally with breadcrumbs and dot with butter, then return to the oven for 20–30 minutes until golden brown.

9. Serve immediately.

CHICKEN RISOTTO

SERVES 4
Approx. 850 ml/1½ pints chicken
or vegetable stock
50 g/2 oz butter
1 medium onion, finely chopped
2 garlic cloves, crushed
350 g/12 oz risotto rice
1 large glass white wine
1 large handful frozen peas, defrosted
Cooked skinless chicken,
torn into strips
Salt and pepper
50 g/2 oz Parmesan cheese, grated

Optional extras:
*200 g/7 oz fresh mushrooms, cleaned and sliced **or***
1 bunch of asparagus, finely chopped with tips intact

1. Heat the stock to boiling point, then simmer.

2. In a separate pan, gently fry the onion and garlic in butter until soft.

3. Stir in the rice, coating the grains with butter.

4 Add the wine, stirring until it's absorbed.

5 Add the mushrooms or asparagus if including.

6 Add the hot stock a ladleful at a time, stirring well between each addition to ensure the liquid is absorbed.

7 When the rice is cooked but firm and the liquid nearly all absorbed (this will take about 20 minutes), add the peas, chicken and seasoning, making sure they are heated through thoroughly.

8 Finally, stir in the Parmesan and serve immediately.

CHICKEN ENCHILADAS

SERVES 5

50 g/2 oz butter
1 large onion, sliced
400 g/14 oz cooked chicken, cut into small pieces
1 red pepper, deseeded and sliced (optional)
1 dessert spoon peri-peri or Cajun spice mix (optional)
5 flour tortillas
1½ tablespoons cornflour
500 ml/18 fl oz milk
225 g/8 oz mature cheddar cheese, grated
Salt and pepper

1 Preheat the oven to 180°C/350°F/gas mark 4.

2 Using a third of the butter, fry the onions until softened, then stir in the chicken, pepper and spice mix (if using).

3 Place a fifth of the mixture into each tortilla, then roll, placing them side-by-side in an oven-proof dish.

4 Combine the rest of the butter with the cornflour and milk in a saucepan and heat gently, whisking all the time to stop lumps forming.

5 Once it comes to the boil, simmer gently for a few minutes, stirring continuously to stop the sauce sticking to the bottom of the pan. Remove from the heat and stir in most of the cheese. Season to taste.

6 Pour the cheese sauce over the rolled tortillas and sprinkle the remaining cheese over the top.

7 Bake in the oven for 25 minutes.

8 Serve with a side salad.

VEGETABLE PIE

SERVES 4
450 g/1 lb cooked leftover vegetables
(e.g. carrots, celeriac, parsnip, potatoes,
sweet potatoes peas or beans)
115 g/4 oz mushrooms
225 g/8 oz onions, chopped
50 g/2 oz butter
25 g/1 oz flour
300 ml/10 fl oz milk
Approx. 85 g/3 oz grated cheese
½ teaspoon dried herbs (optional)
375 g/13 oz pack of ready-rolled puff
or shortcrust pastry
1 egg, beaten

1 Preheat oven to 200°C/400°F/gas mark 6.

2 Fry mushrooms and onions in the butter until soft, then add the rest of the vegetables and mix.

3 Sprinkle the flour over the vegetables, stir well and cook for a few minutes.

4 Gradually add the milk, stirring continuously. Bring to the boil and stir until thick.

5 Fold in the cheese and herbs (if using) and season to taste. Then pour the mixture into a baking dish.

6 Unroll the pastry, lay it on top of the baking dish and trim off any excess with a knife.

7 Pinch the edges of the pastry against the baking dish, brush over with the beaten egg and use a fork to score the top in order to let out the steam.

8 Bake in the oven for 30 minutes or until the pastry is golden.

9 Serve with a green salad.

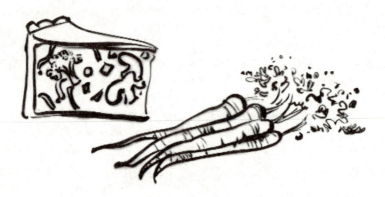

Notorious Women

SHE-WOLF

Medieval French princess Isabella was a legendary beauty, but her husband, King Edward II of England, ignored her throughout their marriage, instead lavishing his attentions on male 'favourites'.

In 1321, while pregnant with her youngest child, Isabella begged her husband to banish his latest favourite, Hugh le Despenser, who was openly using his influence at court to corrupt ends and making the King unpopular by association. Despenser was duly banished, but was recalled a year later. In retaliation, a disgusted Queen Isabella turned against her husband and sought the affections of a nobleman called Roger Mortimer.

Mortimer helped Isabella raise an army, which marched on the King in 1326. The army was successful, the King was imprisoned and Despenser sentenced to death. The deposed King died in jail. Legend has it that Isabella and Mortimer ordered his assassination by the insertion of a red-hot metal rod into his rectum (a not-too-subtle reference to his sexual orientation). Sir Thomas More later described the scene:

> On the night of October 11 while lying in on a bed [the King] was suddenly seized and, while a great mattress . . . weighed him down and suffocated him, a plumber's iron, heated intensely hot, was introduced through a tube into his secret private parts so that it burned the inner portions beyond the intestines.

The Queen and Mortimer ruled as regents for four years until Edward III's accession to the throne at eighteen. As soon as he took power, however, he imprisoned both Isabella and Mortimer. He had Mortimer executed for the murder of his father, before pardoning his mother, who had by then earned the nickname 'the She-Wolf of France'.

THE DESERT QUEEN

Cleopatra's romantic life has been the subject of several Hollywood movies, but her actual marriages were anything but romantic. In fact, the legendary beauty was married twice – both times to her brothers.

At seventeen, Cleopatra became joint ruler of Egypt with her twelve-year-old brother Ptolemy XIII, who was also her husband. Cleopatra had no intention of sharing power, however, and a group of courtiers, affronted by her challenge to the ancient tradition of female rulers being subordinate to male co-rulers, sought to depose her. Cleopatra was forced to flee Egypt.

Ptolemy then made a fatal gaffe by assassinating Julius Caesar's son-in-law, and the Roman was furious. He took over the Palace of Egypt and Cleopatra, spotting an opportunity, presented herself to him in a rolled-up carpet.

Caesar was flattered and took Cleopatra as his mistress, supporting her claim to the Egyptian throne. After a short civil war, Ptolemy XIII was drowned in the Nile and Cleopatra was restored to power with another younger brother, Ptolomy XIV. In accordance with tradition, she then married him, even though he was only eleven years old.

When Julius Caesar was assassinated Cleopatra fled Rome and returned to Alexandria, where she had her brother/husband assassinated and installed her four-year-old son by Caesar, Caesarion, as her co-ruler.

Cleopatra went on to fall in love with Mark Antony, with whom she had a relationship for ten years. Antony killed himself by falling on his own sword after he was defeated by Octavian's army and Cleopatra, captured and facing humiliation, had a poisonous asp smuggled to her in a basket of figs. The snake delivered its fatal bite and Cleopatra died on 12 August 30 BC at the age of just thirty-nine.

BLACK WIDOW

Many women have been dubbed 'black widows' but London-born Dena Thompson did more than most to earn the title. In 2000, Dena appeared in court accused of attempting to murder her third husband, Robert Thompson, whom she had attacked with a baseball bat and knife. She claimed that they'd been involved in a bondage session and that she'd feared for her life. She was acquitted of attempted murder but jailed for conning Mr Thompson and two other men out of £12,000.

The case led to new inquiries into the death of her second husband, Julian Webb, who died suddenly on his thirty-first birthday in June 1994. His body was exhumed and found to contain a large dose of anti-depressants. In the subsequent trial, it emerged that Dena had ground up the pills and added them to her husband's favourite dish – an extra-hot curry – which she served as his birthday meal.

During the trial, more details of her honey-trap cons surfaced. Her first husband had ended up living rough after she'd convinced him they were about to sign a million-pound deal for their toy company but that his life was in danger from the Mafia unless he temporarily disappeared. He consequently signed all his assets over to her, as well as penning a letter in which he falsely confessed to stealing £23,000 from the building society where Dena worked. In addition to these deceits, she told a string of lovers that she was dying in order to con money and holidays out of them.

In December 2003, she was jailed for life for the murder of Julian Webb. Outside the court, a senior detective on the case commented, 'This woman is every man's nightmare. For a decade she has targeted men sexually, financially and physically.

The men of Britain can sleep safe tonight knowing she has been taken off the streets.'

'The most dangerous food is wedding cake.'

AMERICAN PROVERB

ITALIAN TEMPTRESS

Lucrezia Borgia was born in 1480, the daughter of Rodrigo Borgia, Pope Alexander VI. Lucrezia was described as extraordinarily beautiful, with knee-length blonde hair, a clear complexion and natural elegance. By the time she was thirteen she had been betrothed twice, both engagements having been called off by her father. In 1493 she married Giovanni Sforza, a member of a powerful Milanese family that her father was keen to forge an alliance with. Soon afterwards he switched his favour from Milan to Naples and had the union annulled.

A year later Lucrezia married Alfonso of Aragon, the illegitimate son of Alfonso II, but once more his presence became superfluous when Alexander changed sides. He was forced to flee the court and was later murdered on the instruction of Lucrezia's brother, Cesare.

Lucrezia caused a scandal when she appeared with a child – a boy called Giovanni – who had been born in secret. She presented him as her half-brother, but many believe that he was the result of a liaison with her father's messenger or her own brother. Certainly her first husband, Sforza, delighted in spreading rumours of incest.

Her final marriage, to Alfonso d'Este, Prince of Ferrara, was arranged by Cesare in 1501, and as d'Este's bride Lucrezia came into her own, having several children and becoming a respected patron of the arts. When the House of Borgia fell, after her father's death in 1503, she retained her place in European society and died at the age of thirty-nine.

PIRATE QUEEN

Three hundred years before Keira Knightley donned her breeches and set sail on Captain Jack's ship in *Pirates of the Caribbean*, Anne Bonny was doing it for real. This spirited lady was born in Ireland, the illegitimate daughter of a married lawyer and his maid, who fled to America and married when his wronged wife exposed the affair and divorced him.

At sixteen, Anne fell in love with James Bonny, who was either a penniless sailor or pirate, depending on your point of view. Defying her father, who then disowned her, she married James and moved to the pirate's paradise of Nassau, then called New Providence, in the West Indies.

She soon tired of waiting for James to return from his long sea trips and took up with notorious pirate Captain Jack Rackham, also known as Calico Jack, and decided to run away with him. Dressing herself as a man, she joined his crew, and was said to be so vicious with a pistol and cutlass that no one ever questioned her. Legend has it that one man who became suspicious of her gender was dispatched with a sweep of her sword and gutted for good measure.

During one voyage Anne became pregnant, so Captain Jack sailed to Cuba, and left her with friends until the birth. The baby died and Jack took his heartbroken lover back to New

Providence where he took the King's Pardon and gave up piracy. However, James Bonny, who still lived on the island, had the pair arrested and tried for adultery, determined they should

hang. The Governor, who was more lenient, decreed that Anne should merely be flogged and returned to her husband instead. Anne and Jack escaped and fled back to a life of piracy. Along the way they picked up another cross-dressing female called Mary Read, who happily joined their crew and befriended Anne.

In October 1720 their sloop was attacked by a government ship off the coast of Jamaica. The men were too drunk to fight and Anne and Mary were left to defend the ship alone. When they were captured they were spared from hanging as both were pregnant. Just before Captain Jack was hanged he was allowed to see her one last time. 'I'm sorry, Jack,' she told him. 'But if you had fought like a man you would not now be about to die like a dog. Do straighten yourself up!'

Serial Wives

For some women, once just isn't enough. Perhaps it's the dresses, or a passion for wedding cake, but it seems the lessons of love are not always learned the first time round.

ELIZABETH TAYLOR

Screen legend Liz Taylor has enough wedding dresses to open her own bridal boutique, with eight marriages to seven husbands under her belt. She once said, 'My mother says I didn't open my eyes for eight days after I was born, but when I did, the first thing I saw was an engagement ring. I was hooked.'

The London-born actress became a celebrity at the age of twelve, when she starred as a determined child jockey in *National Velvet*, and in 1950, at the tender age of eighteen, she walked down the aisle for the first time. Her marriage, to American hotel heir Conrad 'Nicky' Hilton, lasted less than eight months.

Her second matrimonial outing, to actor Michael Wilding, lasted a little longer at five years and produced two sons, but there was less than a month between her split from Wilding and her marriage to third husband, producer Mike Todd, in

1957. The couple had a daughter, but after thirteen months Liz was tragically widowed when Todd was killed in a plane crash.

The Hollywood legend sought solace in the arms of married singer Eddie Fisher, Mike Todd's best friend. When asked what Todd would have made of her new romance, she reportedly replied, 'What do you expect me to do? Sleep alone?'

Fisher divorced his wife and married Liz in 1959. Four years later, they were in the process of adopting a child when Elizabeth fell for the great love of her life, Richard Burton, on the set of *Cleopatra*. She divorced Fisher in March 1964 and married Burton nine days later. Liz carried on with the adoption of a daughter with the Welsh actor as father. After ten tempestuous years together, Tinseltown's most glamorous couple divorced, only to remarry sixteen months later. This time they lasted only two years.

Husband number six was American politician John Warner and her final marriage was to builder Larry Fortensky, twenty years her junior, whom she met in rehab at the Betty Ford Clinic. The couple married at Michael Jackson's Neverland ranch in 1991 and were divorced five years later.

Despite her high hit-rate, the Oscar-winning star insists that she's an old-fashioned girl at heart: 'I've only slept with men I've been married to,' she once said. 'How many women can make that claim?'

JOAN COLLINS

Joan Collins's stilettos have been down their fair share of aisles, with five marriages to her name. Her first marriage to matinee idol Maxwell Reed ended in 1956 after he tried to sell her to an Arab sheikh.

After another affair, she had a passionate two-year relationship with Warren Beatty, four years her junior at twenty-two, and they became engaged. The marriage wasn't to be, however, and in 1963 Joan walked away to marry singer Anthony Newley, with whom she had two children. They divorced in 1971.

Husband number three was former Apple Records president Ronald Kass. The couple married in 1972 and had a daughter. They divorced in 1983 but remained close friends until Kass's death three years later.

In 1985 Joan embarked on a disastrous marriage to Swedish playboy Peter Holm which lasted a year. When the relationship finally ended a media frenzy began as she famously locked him out of her Beverly Hills mansion. Holm went on to dispute the pre-nuptial agreement he had signed, but lost the case after Joan's lawyer produced Holm's lover as a witness. Holm became a national joke, but walked away with $1 million. In a future autobiography, Joan referred to him only as 'the Swede'.

After a ten-year relationship with art dealer Robin Hurlstone, she met theatre manager Percy Gibson, thirty-three years her junior. The couple married in 2002 at London's Claridge's hotel and Joan dismissed the age gap with characteristic aplomb: 'Look, I'll tell you about the age thing,' joked the then 68-year-old. 'If he dies, he dies!'

ZSA ZSA GABOR

Hungarian socialite and actress Zsa Zsa Gabor once quipped, 'I am a marvellous housekeeper. Every time I leave a man I keep his house.' With nine marriages and several high-profile lovers behind her, that's a lot of real estate!

After divorcing her first husband, Turkish activist Burhan Belge, when she arrived in the US in 1941, she quickly met and married Conrad Hilton (the father of Elizabeth Taylor's first husband). The marriage lasted five years and produced one daughter. While pregnant with her daughter, Zsa Zsa is said to have seen George Sanders on stage and declared that he would be her next husband. She was as good as her word, staying married to him for five years despite conducting a very public affair. In 1962 she married businessman Herbert Hutner three weeks after meeting him, and four years later she repeated the pattern by getting hitched to Joshua S. Cosden six weeks after they met and six days after her divorce.

Her marriage to neighbour Jack Ryan in 1975 lasted less than a year, and a few days after the divorce was granted she wed Michael O'Hara, her divorce lawyer in the case.

Her eighth marriage, to Count Felipe de Alba, lasted just one day in April 1983 and was annulled when it was found to be bigamous. Zsa Zsa was not yet divorced from O'Hara.

Her final marriage was to Frédéric Prinz von Anhalt in 1986. Despite his grand title, the union did not make her European royalty as he had obtained his new name by paying a member of a genuine royal family to legally adopt him.

Zsa Zsa certainly chose her suitors carefully and has amassed a huge fortune. As she famously joked, 'I have never hated a man enough to give his diamonds back.'

LANA TURNER

The stunning Hollywood actress was well known for her many affairs and numerous marriages, which she attributed to the simple fact that 'I liked the boys, and the boys liked me.'

Her first marriage was to band leader Artie Shaw, with whom she eloped after just one date at the age of nineteen. 'After the ceremony we went out to an all-night diner for coffee,' she later recalled. 'Suddenly I realized that my mother had no idea where I was. The taxi drove us to the telegraph office and I wrote out a message: "Got married in Las Vegas. Call you later. Love, Lana."' The stormy relationship lasted just four months and was later referred to by the actress as 'my college education'.

Her marriage to restaurateur Stephen Crane was annulled in 1943 after a year because it was discovered that his divorce had not yet been granted, but a few months after they split the couple remarried. They had a daughter – Lana's only child – but divorced in 1944.

Four years later Lana agreed to marry socialite Henry J. Topping after he dropped a diamond engagement ring into her martini at the 21 Club in Los Angeles. Shortly after the wedding he lost millions through gambling and bad investments and Lana soon grew tired of supporting him. Next she married Lex

Barker, whom she divorced after four years amid allegations of sexual abuse from her daughter.

Lana's affair with mobster Johnny Stompanato went bad, and ended when her fourteen-year-old daughter stabbed him to death to protect her mother during a violent argument in April 1958.

Marriages to rancher Fred May and writer Robert P. Eaton were equally short-lived, and in 1969 she married hypnotist Ronald Pellar, who disappeared six months later with a cheque for $35,000 dollars.

Lana, who died in 1995, summed up her marital history with one poignant comment, 'I expected to have one husband and seven babies. Instead I had seven husbands and one living baby.'

LINDA ESSEX

Linda Essex from Anderson, Indiana holds the record for the greatest number of monogamous marriages, with twenty-three to date. In 1996 she wed the world's most married man, Californian Baptist minister Glynn Wolfe, as a publicity stunt for a television show. She was his twenty-ninth wife, but they spent just one week together before she flew back home. He died in October 1997, a week before their first wedding anniversary.

'I love being married. It's so great to find one special person you want to annoy for the rest of your life.'

RITA RUDNER, COMEDIENNE

WOOK KUNDOR

Wook Kundor married husband number twenty-one, Muhamad Noor Che Musa, in Kuala Lumpar, Malaysia, in 2006. She was reported to be 104 while her new hubby was just 33, an age difference of 71 years! 'I am not after her money as she is poor,' said the blushing bridegroom. 'Before meeting Wook, I never stayed in one place for long.'

BONNIE LEE BAKLEY

Aspiring singer and actress Bonnie Lee Bakley achieved considerably more fame in death than in life after her husband, Hollywood actor Robert Blake, was accused and acquitted of her murder.

Obsessed with celebrity, the girl from New Jersey was determined to marry a star from a young age and claimed to have had a long affair with Jerry Lee Lewis. When she gave birth to a daughter in 1993 she named her Jeri Lee Lewis and accused the singer of being the father, though a DNA test later proved this untrue.

Sadly, Bonnie was an accomplished liar who was married nine times before she met Blake, mainly through lonely hearts scams that enabled her to fleece vulnerable men. After divorcing her second husband, who was also her first cousin and with whom she had two children, she launched her scam by sending nude pictures of herself to men and offering to visit. Between 1984 and 1996 she married seven times, with at least two of the unions lasting less than a week. Through these marriages she amassed enough money to buy several houses before meeting Blake at a party in 1999.

Although she was dating Marlon Brando's son Christian at the time, she slept with Blake, telling him, he later alleged, that she was taking contraceptive pills. When she fell pregnant with his child, Blake agreed to marry her and the couple wed in November 2000. However, Bakley never lived in Blake's house in the San Fernando Valley, but in a small guesthouse next door.

In May 2001, after dinner with her husband at a local restaurant, Bakley was sitting in her car when a gunman shot her through the head. Blake, who had gone back to collect his gun, which he claimed to have left in the restaurant, was not present.

In the controversial trial in 2005, Robert Blake was acquitted of murder, but the judge was not happy and branded the jury 'incredibly stupid'. Later that year a civil court found him liable for the wrongful death of his wife, and Bakley's four children subsequently sued him for $30 million in damages.

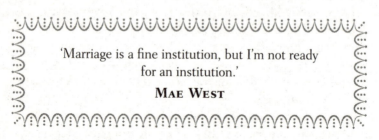

'Marriage is a fine institution, but I'm not ready for an institution.'

MAE WEST

Celebrity Advice

Celebrities seem to suffer from a much higher divorce rate than the rest of us, with showbiz splits filling newspapers and magazines every day. But some married stars have got it right and could teach us all a thing or two about wedded bliss. Here's a guide to a happy marriage – celebrity style.

MAKE TIME FOR EACH OTHER

Hollywood actress Michelle Pfeiffer married *Ally McBeal* producer David E. Kelley in 1993 and they have two children. The *Batman Returns* star likes to keep the marriage alive with regular 'date nights'.

'We tend to our marriage,' she says. 'You have to spend time away from the kids and stay up late and talk, go to the movies or do the crossword puzzle together. My husband and I still have date nights, and I look forward to them all week.'

ROMANTIC GESTURES

Bond star Pierce Brosnan married Keely Shaye Smith in 2001, ten years after the tragic death of first wife, Cassandra. Having brought up three children as a single dad, the dashing actor added two more to his brood with Keely, but still finds time for a romantic gesture.

'I love romance,' he has said. 'I bring Keely breakfast in bed on a tray with a single flower from our garden. I did that when we first started dating, and I still do it.'

> 'There is no substitute for the comfort supplied by the utterly taken-for-granted relationship.'
>
> **IRIS MURDOCH**

KEEP THE ROMANCE ALIVE

Supermodel Heidi Klum and singer husband Seal are a romantic duo. At Christmas 2004, Seal flew Heidi to an igloo on a 14,000-ft glacier in Canada to propose and five months later the couple were married on a private beach in Mexico. The groom even serenaded his stunning bride with a song he'd written for the occasion.

But the romance didn't stop there. Every year, on 10 May, they renew their vows. 'We get married every year at the same place, on the same date,' reveals Heidi. 'It's very romantic.'

KEEP IT SAUCY

Singer Christina Aguilera wed Jordan Bratman in 2005 and has since had their first baby. Jordan's romantic proposal was in a hotel room filled with rose petals, balloons and gift boxes, each one containing a poem he had written. The last box contained a ring and the words, 'Will you do me the honour of being my wife?'

Aside from romance, the couple have a weekly ritual to keep it spicy: 'We have something called Naked Sundays . . . You have to keep marriage alive, spice it up . . . We don't need to go anywhere, we're just with each other. We do everything naked. We cook naked.'

After their Napa Valley marriage the 'Dirrty' singer expressed her respect for her husband by removing all twelve of her body piercings – it must be love.

KEEP YOUR MAN HAPPY

Jerry Hall had four children with rocker Mick Jagger, and in 1990 the couple 'married' in an unofficial Balinese ceremony. But Mick's frequent infidelities led to a split in 1999.

Before they parted, Jerry famously said, 'My mother said it was simple to keep a man, you must be a maid in the living room, a cook in the kitchen and a whore in the bedroom. I said I'd hire the other two and take care of the bedroom bit.'

Sadly, Mick chose to eat out!

STAND BY YOUR MAN

'Bill is a hard dog to keep on the porch,' admitted Hillary Clinton after husband Bill's affair with Monica Lewinsky became public.

Hillary and Bill met at college and married in 1975, but the future President's wandering eye put a constant strain on their marriage. After the scandal caused by his dalliance with White House intern Monica, Hillary admitted that women had always been his 'weakness'.

'I thought he had conquered it. I thought he understood it, but he didn't go deep enough or work hard enough,' she said.

Even during his campaign to reach the White House, his chances were almost ruined when cabaret singer Gennifer Flowers claimed she'd had a twelve-year affair with him.

Hillary came to her husband's rescue, appearing beside him on television to demonstrate her devotion and making the famous reference to the Tammy Wynette classic, 'Stand By Your Man' – 'I'm not sitting here, some little woman standing by her man. I'm sitting here because I love him and I respect him.'

FORGIVE AND FORGET

As Marlene Dietrich succinctly put it, 'Once a woman has forgiven her man, she must not reheat his sins for breakfast.'

> 'Marriage has many pains,
> but celibacy has no pleasures.'
>
> **SAMUEL JOHNSON**

APPRECIATE HIS BEST POINTS

In January 2008, Paul Newman and Joanne Woodward celebrated their fiftieth wedding anniversary. The couple met in 1957 while co-starring in *Long Hot Summer* and married a year later. They have three children.

Throughout their fifty-year marriage, Paul has stuck fast to his famous quote on infidelity: 'Why fool about with a hamburger when you have steak at home.'

Joanne is equally appreciative of her husband's attributes: 'Sexiness wears thin after a while and beauty fades,' she says wisely, 'but to be married to a man who makes you laugh every day, ah, now that's a real treat.'

TALK THINGS THROUGH

Will Smith and wife Jada Pinkett Smith got hitched in 1997 and, as well as their hugely successful Hollywood careers, they have two children of their own and one from Will's previous marriage to keep them busy. Superstar Will knows the secret of a great partnership: 'Really, really good sex. I'm really good at it,' he jokes. 'Also, we talk a lot. Sometimes people hear us talking and think we over-talk situations, but communication is everything.'

COMMUNICATE

Working Girl star Melanie Griffith is a veteran at the marriage game having tied the knot four times. Currently wed to *Zorro* actor Antonio Banderas, she reckons the secret is to let your man know how you feel.

'Let him know you're happy,' she says. 'I smile whenever I see him. He always knows how thrilled I am that he's there with me.'

PURSUE YOUR OWN INTERESTS

After falling off a horse in 1995, Christopher Reeve was paralysed and confined to a wheelchair. Wife Dana became his full-time carer until Christopher's death in 2004, but the lines of communication between them remained the same. 'We have always loved to have conversations and we still do – sometimes lengthy, esoteric and deep; sometimes nostalgic, sometimes just stupid or gossipy,' she said at the time. 'It is so important as a caregiver not to become so enmeshed in the role that you lose yourself. It's neither good for you nor your loved one. I make sure I pursue my own interests and career, and Chris encourages me to do so.'

THE RITUALS OF ROMANCE

As it was wartime, Sir John Mills's 1941 wedding to dramatist Mary Hayley Bell was a rushed civil ceremony, but it proved to be one of the most solid showbusiness marriages in history. The couple finally had their union blessed in a church sixty years later and were married for a total of sixty-four years, until his death in 2005, so who better to divulge the secret of a long marriage?

'Always remembering all the dates, sending a bouquet of flowers every week and keeping the marriage fresh,' said Sir John. 'And we have happy hour every evening at six o'clock. She has her drink, a Horse's Neck, which is a tiny jot of brandy, ginger ale with lemon and ice.'

WORK AT IT

John Travolta and Kelly Preston married in 1991 after meeting on the set of *The Experts* and now have two children. 'You have to keep creating a marriage,' says Kelly. 'We talk about everything. We grow and change together, because nothing ever stays the same; you've got to continue evolving.'

RESPECT YOUR DIFFERENCES

Sleuth star Sir Michael Caine has been married to second wife Shakira since 1973 and says that, despite their differences, they are as close as a couple can get.

'We are so intertwined, my wife and I, that we are almost the same person,' he says. 'We are a partnership. Although we are both Pisces, we are the exact opposite of each other. She's a Kashmiri woman, a Muslim and very gentle and spiritual. I'm exactly the opposite. I'm tough, brutal, mad, a pain in the a***.

'I take care of the tough stuff and she takes care of the gentle stuff, so it works perfectly.

'She is the only person in the world I've ever met who absolutely nobody has anything bad to say about. She's a completely perfect, wonderful person.'

Screen Wives

Beth Gallagher – *Fatal Attraction* (1987)

Played by ANNE ARCHER

THE PLOT: While Beth and her daughter are away visiting relatives, her husband Dan has a one-night stand with the slightly crazy Alex Forrest, played by Glenn Close. When he goes back to his wife and child, Alex begins to stalk him, making the family suffer for Dan's infidelity. She even goes so far as to boil the family's rabbit on their stove.

CHARACTERISTICS: She's patient, forgiving and understanding, but you wouldn't like Beth when she's angry.

MOST MEMORABLE LINE:
'If you ever come near my family again, I'll kill you. Do you understand?'

Morticia Addams – *The Addams Family* (1991)
Played by ANJELICA HOUSTON

THE PLOT: The Addamses live in strange, macabre surroundings with a detached hand as a servant. But their peace and family fortune are threatened when an imposter, posing as their long-lost Uncle Fester, comes to stay.

CHARACTERISTICS: Despite her Gothic garb and weird household, Morticia is a wonderful wife to husband, Gomez, who's still passionately in love with her, and a brilliant mother to her odd offspring, Wednesday and Pugsley.

MOST MEMORABLE LINE:
'Don't torture yourself, Gomez. That's my job.'

Catherine Petersen – *Black Widow* (1987)
Played by THERESA RUSSELL

THE PLOT: A beautiful woman moves from husband to husband, bumping them off and pocketing their money. Federal investigator Alex Barnes (Debra Winger) spots a connection between the mysterious deaths of her victims and sets out to track her down.

CHARACTERISTICS: She's greedy, ruthless and altogether deadly. You certainly wouldn't want your dad introducing her as his new date!

MOST MEMORABLE LINE:
'I'll tell you two things about me: I'm very rich and I'm very wealthy.'

Jane Smith – *Mr & Mrs Smith* (2005)

Played by ANGELINA JOLIE

THE PLOT: If they were lucky enough to be married to Brad Pitt, most women wouldn't spend their days trying to kill him, but John and Jane Smith are trained assassins who have been hired to kill each other.

CHARACTERISTICS: Skilled, deadly and torn between the man she loves and the job she adores. A career change might do her good!

MOST MEMORABLE LINES:
(After showing John the new curtains she's bought.)
JANE: 'If you don't like them we can take them back.'
JOHN: 'All right, I don't like them.'
JANE: [pause] 'You'll get used to them.'

Joanna Eberhart – *The Stepford Wives* (1975)
Played by KATHARINE ROSS

THE PLOT: An urban photographer moves to a tiny Connecticut community with her husband and children, but the quiet suburb doesn't suit her and she takes against the perfect, uncomplaining housewives in the street. After making friends with two of the ladies, she is disturbed when their personalities suddenly change, and on further investigation she discovers a sinister secret behind Stepford's domestic bliss.

CHARACTERISTICS: Joanna is brave and feisty, determined not to fall foul of the strange goings-on in the neighbourhood.

MOST MEMORABLE LINE:
'When you come back, there will be a woman with my name and my face, she'll cook and clean like crazy, but she won't take pictures and *she won't be me*!'

Brenda, Annie and Elise –
The First Wives Club (1996)
Played by BETTE MIDLER,
DIANE KEATON and GOLDIE HAWN

THE PLOT: Three ex-wives, each dumped for a younger model, meet at a friend's funeral and vow to take their revenge. With increasing ingenuity, they plot to hit their former spouses where it hurts – in the pocket.

CHARACTERISTICS: Brenda (Bette Midler) is a struggling single mum; Annie (Diane Keaton) is meek and nervy and Elise (Goldie Hawn) is a vain, ageing actress with a penchant for plastic surgery.

MOST MEMORABLE LINES:
  ELISE: 'I drink because I am a sensitive and highly strung person.'
  BRENDA: 'No, that's why your co-stars drink.'

  ELISE: 'It's the nineties; plastic surgery is like good grooming.'

Corie Bratter – *Barefoot in the Park* (1967)
Played by JANE FONDA

THE PLOT: A young ambitious lawyer, played by Robert Redford, marries Corie, whose only ambition is to have fun. They move into a tiny apartment five floors up in the centre of New York, and as he works to secure their future, she devotes her waking hours to getting him to join in with her various japes.

CHARACTERISTICS: She's lovable, goofy and tons of fun, but Corie would drive most men mad.

Most memorable line:
'Paul, I think I'm gonna be a lousy wife. But don't be angry with me. I love you very much – and I'm very sexy!'

Kay Miniver – *Mrs Miniver* (1942)
Played by **Greer Garson**

The plot: Greer Garson won an Oscar for her role as a middle-class housewife coping with life in World War II. With her husband off assisting with the Dunkirk landings and her son in the RAF, Mrs Miniver refuses to let the conflict affect her everyday life. At one point she finds a wounded German pilot in her garden and takes him inside for something to eat before calmly disarming him and having him arrested.

Characteristics: Brave, practical, pragmatic and reliable, Mrs Miniver was a shining example to wartime women and a great way of boosting morale. In fact, the film's closing lines (spoken by the vicar) were so powerful that President Franklin Roosevelt ordered them to be printed on millions of leaflets to be dropped over Nazi-occupied Europe: 'This is the people's war! It is our war! We are the fighters! Fight it then! Fight it with all that is in us, and may God defend the right.'

Most memorable line:
'I'm practically unprepared!'
(Spoken as Greer Garson accepted the Best Actress Oscar for the role. She went on to make a seven-minute speech – the longest in the history of the Academy Awards.)

Husbands from Hell

For every Rhett Butler there's a rat. Life in the movies isn't all romance, roses and happily-ever-afters. Here are a few screen spouses you wouldn't want to know!

Lester Burnham – *American Beauty* (1999)
Played by KEVIN SPACEY

THE PLOT: A suburban father in an outwardly happy marriage goes through a mid-life crisis that culminates in a deep infatuation with one of his daughter's friends.

BIGGEST FAULTS: It can't be too thrilling to have a husband who spends his time fantasizing about a teenager. Mind you, his wife is too busy having a fling with her business rival to notice.

MOST MEMORABLE LINES:
(After Lester catches his wife cheating on him with Buddy King.)
CAROLYN: 'Uh, Buddy, this is my . . .'
LESTER: 'Her husband. We've met before, but something tells me you're going to remember me this time.'

Martin Burney – *Sleeping with the Enemy* (1991)

Played by PATRICK BERGIN

THE PLOT: Laura and Martin appear to their friends to have the perfect marriage, but behind closed doors Laura (Julia Roberts) lives in fear of her brutal and abusive husband. To get away, Laura fakes her own death and sets up a new life with a new identity, but when Martin finds out his wife isn't dead, he vows she soon will be.

BIGGEST FAULTS: He's manipulative, creepy, abusive and violent. Not much going for him in the husband of the year awards.

MOST MEMORABLE LINE:
'I can't live without you. And I won't let you live without me.'

Jack Torrance – *The Shining* (1980)

Played by JACK NICHOLSON

THE PLOT: After Jack gets a job as a caretaker he moves his family to an isolated hotel, closed for the winter. However, evil spirits lurk in the building and soon Jack becomes possessed.

BIGGEST FAULTS: After listening to the ghost of a waiter, he attempts to 'correct' his wife and son by chopping them into small pieces.

MOST MEMORABLE LINE:
'Here's Johnny!'

Ennis Del Mar – *Brokeback Mountain*
(2005)
Played by HEATH LEDGER

THE PLOT: After warming each other up on a cold night in the mountains, ranch hands Ennis and Jack contrive regular get-togethers to rekindle their forbidden love.

BIGGEST FAULTS: He's a nice guy, but his frustrations mean he's not a great husband. Unable to accept the way he feels about Jack, he lies to his wife and regularly takes off on 'fishing trips' with his lover.

MOST MEMORABLE LINE:
'Mexico? Hell, Jack, you know me, about all the travelin' I ever done is round a coffee pot lookin' for the handle.'

Guy Woodhouse – *Rosemary's Baby*
(1968)
Played by JOHN CASSAVETES

THE PLOT: A young couple move to a new apartment where they befriend a neighbouring older couple. As her husband grows closer to their neighbours, Rosemary is increasingly suspicious of their behaviour and the weird things happening around them. After she has a strange dream, in which she is raped, she finds she's pregnant and begins to suspect that her growing baby is part of a satanic plot.

BIGGEST FAULTS: As if sacrificing his wife's sanity in the name of devil-worship isn't enough!

MOST MEMORABLE LINES:
  ROSEMARY: 'You had me while I was out?'
  GUY: 'It was kinda fun in a necrophile sort of way.'

Sweeney Todd – *Sweeney Todd*
(2007)
Played by JOHNNY DEPP

THE PLOT: After being forcibly separated from his wife and child by a jealous judge who deports him to Australia, Benjamin Barker returns to London under the assumed name Sweeney Todd and sets about slitting the throats of all those who have wronged him and sticking them in a pie.

BIGGEST FAULTS: His devotion to his wife and child is admirable and tragic, but he takes the idea of revenge a little too far.

MOST MEMORABLE LINE:
  'I can guarantee the closest shave you'll ever know.'

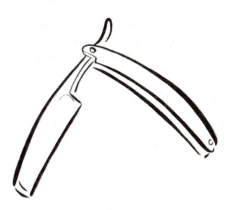

Jake La Motta – *Raging Bull*
(1980)

Played by ROBERT DE NIRO

THE PLOT: Jake is a demon in the ring, a prizefighter who can obliterate any opponent. Away from the ring, however, he's an emotional wreck whose dealings with his family, especially his wife, are tainted by the same rage that makes him a great boxer.

BIGGEST FAULTS: His paranoia and jealousy drives a wedge between himself and his wife Vickie.

MOST MEMORABLE LINE:
'I got these small hands. I got a little girl's hands.'

Homer Simpson – *The Simpsons Movie*
(2007)

Voiced by DAN CASTELLANETA

THE PLOT: After Homer tips toxic waste into Springfield's water supply, the town is sealed under a huge glass dome and threatened with destruction, leading the Simpson family to become fugitives.

BIGGEST FAULTS: He's lovable but he's also lazy and incurably dumb.

MOST MEMORABLE LINE:
'D'oh!'

A Woman Scorned

'Heaven has no rage like love to hatred turned,
nor hell a fury like a woman scorned.'

WILLIAM CONGREVE

The Bardsley playwright who wrote these oft misquoted words in his tragedy *The Mourning Bride* clearly knew a thing or two about women. Many a cheating husband has fallen foul of his enraged wife, forgetting the cardinal rule: never upset the person who knows you best. You can guarantee she know exactly how to hit you where it hurts!

BED AND BOARD

An unfaithful husband in Birmingham, England had his indiscretions put on display in December 2006 when his furious wife hired a billboard and paid for a giant ad. Apparently, following the advice of local radio presenters, she raided the coffers to have the following message plastered on a hoarding in the city centre:

> To my 'dear husband' Mark and my 'best friend' Shelley, you are the most despicable, deceitful people I have ever met. I know what you did and I'm disgusted. I've changed the locks, Mark, burnt your clothes and emptied OUR joint account – to pay for this poster. You deserve each other.

The ad, which was spotted by thousands of drivers and pedestrians, was signed Jane Doe, the American phrase for an unidentified woman.

A LADY SEES RED

When Lady Sarah Graham-Moon discovered her husband, Sir Peter, had been less than a gentleman, she turned on the things he loved the most.

First she let rip with the kitchen scissors, cutting one arm from each of his expensive Savile Row suits, of which there were thirty-two. Next came his beloved BMW, which was soon wearing several litres of white paint after she found it parked outside his mistress's house.

Knowing how Sir Peter loved his vintage claret, she cheered up her Chelsea neighbours by depositing the contents of his wine cellar on their doorsteps along with the morning milk.

Finally, she ripped pictures and clothing belonging to her husband and made 'a big sculpture'.

'I'm normally quite in control of my emotions,' said the new avenger. 'In fact, I am quite shocked by what I have done.'

CHINESE BURN

A businessman's wife in China was bent on revenge when her husband walked out. She gathered the entire stock of mobile phones from the shop they owned and set fire to the lot. The damage came to £21,000.

PR DISASTER

The wife of PR company boss Paul Evans was not in the best of moods when she decided to humiliate her husband by email. The missive entitled 'Time to 'Fess up!' was sent from his laptop to everybody listed in his contacts. It said:

> I, Paul Owen Evans, am a snivelling, cheating, lying, arrogant little piece of shit. No, that's not right, I'm worse than that: I'm a despicable, deceitful, dodgy, DICKHEAD who doesn't reserve this attitude just for his wife. Oh yes, one more thing – I've got an extremely small penis that couldn't excite a woman's nostril let alone anything else. Thus endeth my confession. Regards. Paul Evans.

Paul was at a car launch in Barcelona at the time and the email went to all his influential associates at various car firms, as well as all his friends.

ANYTHING YOU CAN DO . . .

In 2006, Pavla Topolánek, wife of the Czech prime minister, was not happy when a tabloid newspaper reported an affair between her husband and the 36-year-old deputy leader of Parliament,

Lucie Talmanová, and as revenge she decided to stand for election – as a candidate for the opposition.

Mirek Topolánek said he was 'surprised' by his wife's decision to stand for Politika 21 under the slogan 'No to political arrogance', but that he wasn't upset. Other members of his Civil Democrat party, however, were left fuming and suggested that Pavla would do better to support her husband than harbour ambitions of her own

Mrs Topolánek, in turn, claimed that she wanted to break the 'traditional cliché' that prevented wives from pursuing their own careers.

Unfortunately, her revenge was short-lived as she didn't make it past the first round of votes. Her husband now lives with Miss Talmanová.

JOCK SHOCKED

British shock jock Tim Shaw got more than he bargained for when he told glamour model Jodie Marsh that he'd happily leave his wife and two kids for her. Long-suffering Hayley Shaw, listening at home, decided on instant revenge by putting his Lotus Esprit sports car up for sale on eBay.

Determined to do the deal before he got home from his show on Kerrang! radio, she wrote in her description: 'I need to get rid of this car immediately – ideally in the next 2–3 hours before my cheating a***hole husband gets home to find it gone and all his belongings in the street. I am the registered owner and I have the log book. Please only buy if you can pick up tonight.'

The auction was over in five minutes and three seconds when the car, worth around £25,000, was sold for 50p.

Shaw had often upset his wife with his comments on the

show, and on one occasion, while she was heavily pregnant, he claimed he fantasized about his wife's sister while making love. When she rang up in tears to complain, he put her on air.

'I am sick of him disrespecting this family for the sake of his act,' Hayley told a Birmingham newspaper after selling the Lotus. 'The car is his pride and joy, but the idiot put my name on the log book, so I just sold it. I didn't care about the money. I just wanted to get him back.'

THE UNKINDEST CUT

The most famous wifely revenge of all is that of Lorena Bobbitt. In 1993, after another drunken fumble from husband John Wayne Bobbitt, she took a twelve-inch steak knife and cut off his manhood as he lay in bed.

She then ran out of the house, drove off in the car and threw the severed member out of the window. It was later recovered and reattached.

Lorena's defence? 'He always has an orgasm and doesn't wait for me. It's unfair.'

Amazingly, Lorena was acquitted of malicious wounding, although she did spend some time in a mental institution. Not so amazingly, the couple are now divorced.

'Sometimes I wonder if men and women really suit each other. Perhaps they should live next door and just visit now and then.'

KATHARINE HEPBURN

MEDIA MASTERS

When *Spectator* columnist and editor of the *Today* programme Rod Liddle dumped his new bride for his mistress, she decided to beat him at his own game by writing about it in the national press.

In all, she wrote nine columns, dubbing them her 'divorce diaries', in which she detailed her husband's betrayals. 'In the scheme of how hurt I was about what he'd done to me – leaving our honeymoon early to spend a week with his mistress, lying to me for months and months about the affair – it just seemed like a very small revenge,' she said.

French actress Isabel Adjani employed a similar tactic when she discovered her fiancé, musician Jean-Michel Jarre, had been playing his tubular bells elsewhere by using the cover of *Paris Match* magazine to announce to the world, and him, that their engagement was off.

IT'S CURTAINS FOR THIS MARRIAGE

This appears to be an urban myth as the lady in question is never identified, but it's a great story nonetheless.

After finding out about her husband's affair and ending their marriage, the spurned wife prepared to move out of the marital home and consoled herself with a last supper of shrimps and caviar. She found a novel way to dispose of the fishy leftovers by stuffing them inside the hollow curtain rods all over the house.

Hubby immediately moved his new girlfriend in and everything was peachy for the first few days . . . until an awful smell started to waft around the house. They cleaned and mopped until the place was sparkling, they aired it regularly and checked for dead vermin. Rentokil came and found nothing. Friends stopped calling round and the couple became so desperate they put the house up for sale.

After some time on the market, and slashing the price several times, hubby got a call from his ex-wife. She told him she missed her home terribly and would consider reducing her divorce settlement if she could have the house.

Delighted with the arrangement, and assuming she knew nothing about the smell, he jumped at the chance and gave her the house at a tenth of its market value.

A few weeks later the papers were signed and the man and his girlfriend were pleased as punch as they watched the removal men pack everything to take to their new home, including the curtain rods!

True Romance

When Anna Kozlov returned to the Siberian village where she grew up she got the shock of her life. Also visiting that day was Boris, the man she had married sixty years earlier. The last time she'd seen him had been three days into their marriage, when she'd kissed him goodbye as he went to rejoin his Red Army unit. Tragically, Anna's family fell victim to Stalin's purges and were sent into internal exile, and despite Boris's desperate searches, her returning husband could find no trace of her.

Sixty years on, at eighty years of age, Boris made the journey to Borovlyanka to visit his parents' grave. When he arrived he saw his long-lost bride standing outside her old house. 'I ran up to her and said, "My darling, I've been waiting for you for so long. My wife, my life . . ."'

'I thought my eyes were playing games with me,' Anna said. 'I saw this familiar-looking man approaching me, his eyes gazing at me. My heart jumped. I knew it was him. I was crying with joy.'

The couple met in 1946, but Anna's entire family were forced into exile after her father refused to work on a collective farm. Eventually, both Anna and Boris lost hope of finding each other again and married other people, although Boris, who pursued a writing career, still dedicated a book to his lovely Anna.

By the time they were reunited, both were widowed and anxious to make up for lost time. 'I couldn't take my eyes off her,' said Boris. 'Yes, I had loved other women when we were separated. But she was the true love of my life.'

Boris proposed once more, and although Anna wasn't keen to wed again at her advanced age, Boris talked her round.

'"What's the point?" I said, "We can just live together the rest of our lives." But he insisted. I never thought I'd be a bride at my age, but it was my happiest wedding,' she said.

'Since we found each other again, I swear we haven't had a single quarrel. We've been parted for so long and who knows how much time is left for us, so we don't want to lose time on arguing.'

Mughal Emperor Shah Jahan of India was heartbroken when his wife, Mumtaz Mahal, died in childbirth, so he decided to build the most lavish of memorials to her. Twenty thousand labourers worked for twenty-two years from 1634 to complete the building, which was named the Taj Mahal in her honour.

Queen Victoria's wedding to Prince Albert in 1840 was a grand affair. The Queen was dressed in white satin trimmed with orange blossoms and studded with diamonds, set off by huge diamond earrings and a matching necklace. The wedding breakfast was held at Buckingham Palace and the cake was a wonder to behold – the first tier had a circumference of more than nine feet and the second was supported by two pedestals. On the second tier a sculpture of Britannia gazed upon models of the royal newlyweds, and at their feet were two turtledoves, symbolizing purity and innocence, and a dog to represent fidelity and devotion. Sculpted cupids completed the tableau, one of which was writing the date of the wedding on a tablet.

When Mexican Octavio Guillen proposed to girlfriend Adriana Martinez in 1902 they were both fifteen. By the time she got her long-awaited wedding day they were eighty-two! The pair put the wedding off time and time again until they finally tied the knot in June 1969. Theirs was the world's longest engagement at sixty-seven years.

A romantic marriage proposal sparked a UFO scare in the quiet Bavarian town of Plattling in May 2008.

The local police received several calls about weird lights drifting across the night sky near the River Isar, but when they arrived to investigate, there wasn't an alien in sight, only a young couple having a romantic evening.

The 29-year-old man had decided to propose to his 27-year-old girlfriend and, to set the mood, had released fifty glowing paper lanterns into the air. He had cleared it with the aviation authority first, but hadn't thought to tell the police.

Luckily, his gesture was appreciated by the young lady in question, who said yes.

For John Santino and Toni Wilson, their big day was wetter than most, but there were no complaints about the weather since it was the largest ever underwater wedding.

The keen divers tied the knot 11 feet below the surface in the waters off the Rainbow Beach Club in Frederiksted, St Croix, in the US Virgin Islands in September 2003. There were 106 people there, including the bride and groom.

Under her scuba gear Toni wore a white Lycra top and shorts with a veil weighed down with shells and glass, while John wore a pair of black shorts and a top with a bow tie.

'As a girl, you always imagine what your wedding would be like, but I have to admit that I never imagined it would be held underwater,' said the dripping bride. 'John was the instructor that certified me a year ago, and we just felt that with scuba diving being such a big part of his life, it would be great to hold the wedding underwater.'

India's first Prime Minister, Jawaharlal Nehru, married Kamala Kaul in 1916 and the wedding festivities lasted six weeks. There were badminton and tennis marathons, dozens of dinner parties, musical performances and poetry readings before the groom and male guests trekked into the mountains for a month-long hunting trip.

A mountain lion that attacked a walker in Prairie Creek Redwoods State Park near San Francisco wasn't banking on the determination of its victim's loving wife.

In January 2007, Jim and Nell Hamm were hiking in the area when the deadly predator struck. Nell picked up a four-inch log and started battering the animal, which still refused to let go of her husband's head. Next she took a pen and started jabbing the lion in the eye, but the pen broke so she returned to her original weapon.

Eventually the lion released its grip and turned on Nell, who waved her weapon and screamed at it until it slowly backed away.

The heroic 65-year-old then refused to leave her injured husband alone and forced him to get up and walk another quarter of a mile to the head of the trail, where she gathered branches to protect them from further attack while they waited for rangers to arrive.

'My concern was to get Jim out of there,' she said. 'I told him, "Get up. Get up, walk," and he did.'

The seventy-year-old was treated for lacerations to his head and body, but thanks to Nell, he survived to celebrate the couple's fiftieth wedding anniversary a few months later.

His devoted wife is under no illusion that, had he been alone, Jim would not have come out alive: 'We fought harder than we ever have to save his life,' she said. 'And we fought together.'

Extreme sports fan Mark Brailsford arrived at his 2008 wedding in Derbyshire, England in style – he abseiled down the church tower. He had proposed to girlfriend Lena after they climbed a mountain in Mauritius together. The bride wasn't going to be outdone on her big day, though – she arrived in a canoe.

Married couple Thomas and Nancy Beatie always dreamed of starting a family – so he got pregnant. Thomas started life as

Tracy, but had a sex change and was legally declared a man, although he kept his reproductive organs. Nancy, whom he wed in 2002, had already had a hysterectomy, so he decided to have the child they wanted through artificial insemination.

'Our desire to work hard, buy our first home and start a family was nothing out of the ordinary. Until we decided that I would carry our child,' he wrote.

His pregnancy came as something of a shock to his neighbours in Bend, Oregon, where they had only ever known him as a man!

Thomas gave birth to a baby girl in July 2008.

Swans are well known for their long and faithful relationships, but black swan Petra made headlines in 2006 when she fell for a plastic pedal boat.

Zookeepers in the German town of Münster released Petra on a local lake where she became besotted with the boat, which was shaped like a white swan.

The love-struck bird refused to be parted from her new flame or mingle with her feathered friends. In the winter she even refused to migrate, so Petra and her pedalo had to be housed in a heated enclosure. The new romance sparked a huge tourist trade as locals sold souvenirs in the shape of the odd couple.

A rare Australian black swan, nicknamed Bruce, eventually succeeded in turning Petra's head and the pair began to build a nest, but Bruce proved to be a feathered fly-by-night and soon took off with another mate.

Poor Petra was once more distraught, until she was reunited with her first love, the swan-shaped pedalo.

Showbiz Whirlwinds

The ink is barely dry on the marriage certificate when some celebrity newlyweds are signing a divorce petition. Here are a few disastrous unions, which go to prove the age-old adage, 'Marry in haste, repent at leisure.'

JENNIFER LOPEZ AND CRIS JUDD

The couple's short-lived marriage ended when singer Lopez began publicly dating Ben Affleck.

WED: September 2001
SPLIT: June 2002
DURATION: 9 months

SHANNEN DOHERTY AND ASHLEY HAMILTON

The *Beverly Hills 90210* star married actor George Hamilton's son two weeks after meeting him.

WED: September 1993
SPLIT: February 1994
DURATION: 5 months

CARMEN ELECTRA AND DENNIS RODMAN

Nine days after a quickie Las Vegas wedding ceremony, Dennis filed for an annulment, but the couple tried again and this time it worked – for a few months!

WED: November 1998
SPLIT: March 1999
DURATION: 5 months

CHARLIE SHEEN AND DONNA PEELE

The actor's wedding on his thirtieth birthday turned into a mid-life crisis.

WED: September 1995
SPLIT: February 1996
DURATION: 4 months, 24 days

RENÉE ZELLWEGER AND KENNY CHESNEY

Their dream wedding on a beach in the Virgin Islands soon turned into a nightmare and Renée filed for an annulment.

WED: May 2005
SPLIT: September 2005
DURATION: 4 months, 7 days

LISA MARIE PRESLEY AND NICOLAS CAGE

Elvis fan Cage was 'all shook up' by his brief marriage to The King's daughter.

WED: August 2002
SPLIT: November 2002
DURATION: 3 months, 15 days

ERNEST BORGNINE AND ETHEL MERMAN

When the Hollywood couple split after thirty-two days of wedded bliss, Johnny Carson quipped, 'And they said it wouldn't last!'

WED: June 1964
SPLIT: July 1964
DURATION: 32 days

~~~~~~~~~~~~~~~~~~~~~~~~~~~~~~~~~~~~~~

DREW BARRYMORE AND JEREMY THOMAS

The actress married Jeremy Thomas in March 1994 and soon discovered that the union of a recovering alcoholic and a bar owner is not a match made in heaven.

  WED: March 1994
  SPLIT: April 1994
  DURATION: 30 days

CHER AND GREGG ALLMAN

The 'Turn Back Time' singer wished she could do just that after her whirlwind Las Vegas wedding to Allman.

  WED: July 1975
  SPLIT: July 1975
  DURATION: 9 days

DENNIS HOPPER AND MICHELLE PHILLIPS

The Mamas and the Papas singer Michelle soon found she didn't want to play house.

  WED: October 1970
  SPLIT: November 1970
  DURATION: 9 days

~~~~~~~~~~~~~~~~~~~~~~~~~~~~~~~~~~~~~~

BRITNEY SPEARS AND JASON ALEXANDER

Singer Britney wed childhood pal Jason after a night out in Vegas because they wanted to do 'something wild'. She filed for an annulment shortly after.

WED: January 2006
SPLIT: January 2006
DURATION: 55 hours

RUDOLPH VALENTINO AND JEAN ACKER

The legendary lover's wedding night didn't go as planned when his new bride locked him out of the bridal suite.

WED: November 1919
SPLIT: November 1919
DURATION: 6 hours

'A deal is a deal. To me that says it all.
Marriage is for keeps.'

COURTENEY COX
ON MARRIAGE TO DAVID ARQUETTE

Modern Manners

In days gone by, when a marriage came to an end there would be an emotional chat (or furious row) and the very least a wife could expect would be a long and heartfelt letter in the post.

Modern-day manners, however, mean you're just as likely to be dumped by hastily typed email or text message, as these cases demonstrate.

THE COOK REPORT

The late Labour politician Robin Cook was at Heathrow airport with his wife Margaret when he announced his intention to leave her for his mistress, Gaynor Regan.

The Cooks, who had been married for twenty-eight years and had two sons, were on their way to Boston for a holiday to celebrate their marriage in the wake of a rocky patch. As they drove to the airport, however, the then Foreign Secretary received a call to say that his affair was about to be revealed in the press.

Margaret was left reeling from shock when her husband told her the holiday was cancelled and immediately issued a statement to the press saying that he was leaving his wife for his mistress.

TOXIC TEXT

Men aren't the only ones to take the easy way out. Britney Spears dumped hubby Kevin Federline by text while he was in

Canada. To make matters worse, poor K-Fed was being followed around by cameras from the MuchMusic channel at the time and had been waxing lyrical about his wife and their two kids in interviews all day.

On camera, the unwitting rapper was seen receiving a text that made him visibly upset. He then turned his camera off and disappeared for half an hour.

YOU'VE GOTTA HAVE SOUL

When the Godfather of Soul, James Brown, chose to break up with his young wife, Tommy Rae Hynie, he took out a full-page ad in the entertainment magazine *Variety*. The 2003 split was announced alongside a photograph of the happy couple at Disney World with their two-year-old son, James Joseph Brown II.

The ad claimed that due to a 'heavy, demanding tour schedule, they have decided to go their separate ways. There are no hard feelings, just a mutual show-business decision made by both parties.' Despite a very public divorce, Tommy Rae claimed she was still married to the star at the time of his death in 2006.

Conversely, Hollywood actor Richard Gere took out an ad in the UK broadsheet, *The Times*, in 1994 to proclaim that his marriage to Cindy Crawford was strong and the couple were planning to have a family together. Seven months later they announced their split.

'The reason for much matrimony is patrimony.'

OGDEN NASH, POET

GET THE FAX RIGHT

When Phil Collins fell in love with Swiss interpreter Orianne Cevey and decided to split with his second wife, Jill Tavelman, reports claimed he broke the news by fax. The singer has since denied this, saying he sent a fax to his wife because she kept putting the phone down and he needed to make arrangements about visiting their daughter, Lily.

'It wasn't happening. She kept putting the phone down. So I sent her a fax, telling her what I was trying to tell her on the phone. That was the fax,' he said. 'But just to fax her telling her I wanted a divorce? How could someone do that? I couldn't. I did not do that. But you can't unwrite what's been written, and I've just got to live with it.'

WIKID

Canadian political pundit Rachel Marsden had a brief relationship with Jimmy Wales, the co-founder of the famous Wikipedia, at the beginning of 2008. Miss Marsden discovered the affair was over when she logged on to Wikipedia to find that Jimmy had posted a statement on the site saying, 'I am no longer involved with Rachel Marsden.'

She responded in a similarly modern fashion by putting his dirty laundry up for sale on eBay.

PAINFUL REMINDER

Steelworker Alan Jenkins went to great lengths to show his common-law wife, Lisa, how much he loved her – by having her face tattooed on his back.

After twenty hours of painful tattoo work, a process he described as 'like nails being dragged across an open wound', he was proud of the giant portrait of Lisa and their two daughters.

Unfortunately, Lisa then fell in love with another man and kicked Alan out of the house. Unable to afford expensive laser treatment to remove the tattoo, he now carries around a permanent reminder of their relationship. It gives new meaning to the idea of your ex being constantly on your back.

PRIVATE AND CONFIDENTIAL

American novelist Robert Olen Butler was devastated when his wife, Elizabeth Dewberry, left him for media mogul Ted Turner, and sent an email to a select few of his students at Florida State University to inform them of the split.

The email included the theory that Elizabeth was attracted to Mr Turner because he reminded her of the grandfather who had abused her as a child, although he was careful to point out that his love rival was not abusive in any way. After writing that his wife of twelve years was not likely to be Mr Turner's only girlfriend, he concluded, 'You need not keep this to yourself, since I am not up to the task of telling this story over and over.'

The story went a little further than predicted, however, when it was picked up by a US gossip website, which published it in full, labelling it the 'insanest email ever'.

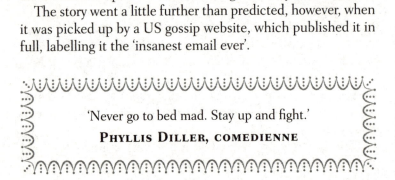

'Never go to bed mad. Stay up and fight.'
PHYLLIS DILLER, COMEDIENNE

Changing Times

Depending on your relationship, the honeymoon period can last between a fortnight (when you actually get back from your honeymoon) to forty years (in extremely rare circumstances). However, change is the one constant in life and it is inevitable that your marriage will suffer knocks and bumps along the way.

THE NEW BABY

Should you choose to become parents, the biggest transition you will go through is when your family grows from two to three.

A baby is time-consuming, tiring and demands all your attention. No matter how busy you thought you were before the patter of tiny feet arrived, it will be nothing compared to this. There may be days when you barely have time to shower, so putting dinner on the table and cleaning the house soon goes out the window.

At this point husbands, no matter how helpful, often feel neglected. It's not that he expects to be waited on hand and foot, but he may feel starved of your attention and your affection, because the baby seems to be getting it all.

Here are a few tips for getting through it.

Spend time together
It's unrealistic to say you should plan time together, unless you accept you need back-up. If parents, neighbours or friends offer you a couple of hours' respite, take it. Go for lunch or for an evening meal and give yourself a chance to talk to each other –

and not just about the baby. If that's not possible, set some time aside in the evening, when the baby is sleeping, to catch up.

Walk and talk

If you're taking the baby out in the buggy, ask your husband to join you. Small children are usually content when they're being wheeled along, so you can both chat while you walk. It's also good exercise and helps shift any post-pregnancy weight. Alternatively, agree on other pursuits that include all three of you, such as swimming.

Involve him

It's all too easy, especially if you are breastfeeding, to take over all the baby care yourself. But remember, your husband needs to take part in everyday jobs, such as nappy-changing and bathing, as well as just playing with the baby for ten minutes when he gets home from work. If you pick up the baby every time he or she cries and leave your husband standing by feeling useless, he will start to feel shut out.

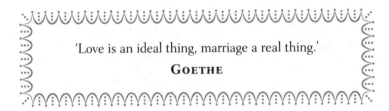

'Love is an ideal thing, marriage a real thing.'

GOETHE

Tackle the tiredness

Feeling permanently exhausted is a common complaint for parents during the first few months of a baby's life, but it can also make you grumpy and hard to live with. If possible, sleep during the day to compensate for any loss of sleep at night. When baby settles down for a nap, don't worry about the washing up, get some well-earned rest instead. Scientific research by NASA had shown that even a nap of 20–30 minutes in the middle of the day increases brain function and relieves stress.

Even if you are breastfeeding, night-time feeds should be a shared responsibility – up to a point. If he has to get up at six every morning and go to work, then he can't spend half the night dealing with a fractious infant. Equally, if you have gone weeks without a full night's sleep, he needs to step in. Express milk or make up bottles in advance, and don't wait until the middle of the night to tell him it's his turn.

Sleep deprivation is defined as getting less than four hours of uninterrupted sleep, so if the baby is waking up every two to three hours, try to do alternate feeds. Remember, the sleepless stage won't last for ever. All babies are different, but the following table shows the average sleep times of a newborn:

AGE	SLEEPING TIME
1–8 weeks	2–4 hours
8–10 weeks	4–6 hours
10–12 weeks	6–8 hours

Keep interest alive

Nine times out of ten, a new mum will be at home with the newborn long after the dad has returned to work. Although he adores his newborn child and can't wait to get home at the end of the day, not every one of his waking thoughts will be about his son or daughter, and neither should yours. Join a mother-and-baby group, get out and about with friends, go shopping, have lunch and arrange things to keep yourself occupied. Even watching the news while feeding the baby will give you something else to think about. That way your conversation will be livelier when he gets home, instead of a constant, weary stream of, 'He hasn't stopped crying all day.'

Socialize

No matter how happy you are together, it's important to mix with other couples. Just because you have a new baby doesn't mean you have to stop being sociable. You can't go to the pub every weekend, and a meal out needs military planning, so invite people round for dinner. It doesn't have to be time-consuming to prepare – make something quick and easy or get a takeaway. Your friends are there for your company, not your cuisine.

OLDER CHILDREN

As your children grow, they make different demands on your time and energy. Whether it's getting their school stuff ready, making packed lunches or taking them to the park, there are never enough hours in the day. The chances are that you may have returned to work, making the juggling act even harder. Dealing with the everyday things together can make your marriage stronger and create more time for each other.

Parent time

As soon as your children are old enough to understand, introduce the concept of 'parent time'. This should be at least twenty minutes, perhaps after dinner, when you sit and chat as a couple and they know that they must go and play quietly. At first you may find they constantly interrupt, but stay firm and by the time they are four they will respect the need for you to have grown-up talk.

Don't feel guilty about getting a babysitter when you want a night out together, or about going away for the weekend and leaving the children with willing grandparents. If your relationship is happy and healthy, the kids will benefit.

Family time

Rather than one of you keeping the children in check while the other goes about their work or chores, try to plan family days. You will all appreciate having a day out together at the zoo or park, or going on a picnic, and the fact that you can share in your children's fun together will also give your relationship a boost.

Organization

If you and your husband can get into a routine during the busiest times of day it will cut stress dramatically. For instance, in the morning, when everyone is getting ready to leave the house, he could be helping the children clean their teeth while you make their lunches. When school means a different activity every day, try to get the necessary kit together the night before, once they have gone to bed. At bedtime, take it in turns to get them ready and read bedtime stories while the other clears away the dishes.

Delegation

You might be superwoman, but if you try to do everything, you'll drive yourself nuts and end up shouting at the rest of the family. Impress upon your kids from an early age that they must help Mummy and Daddy around the house. Start with easy tasks, such as taking the salt and pepper to the dinner table and putting the place mats out, and progress to washing dishes, drying up, and so on.

Consistent care

One of the major friction points in families is the issue of consistency when it comes to care and discipline. It's confusing for a child when Mummy says no and Daddy says yes, and it can cause resentment between parents. Before you take a stance on an issue, try to discuss it with your partner and stick to what you agree. If that is impractical, then make sure he knows what decision you have made and what you have told the children.

TEENAGERS

They can't help it. Teenagers are grumpy, grouchy, unreasonable human beings who can drive both parents to distraction. If the house is full of raised voices, it can affect your marriage as well as your relationship with the kids.

Stay on the same side
Teenagers are past masters at playing one parent off against another and pushing the boundaries is their *raison d'être*. Never undermine one another in front of your teenager, and if your husband has grounded a child for a misdemeanour, don't let him or her go out behind his back, or spoil them to make up for it.

Discuss things in private
Whatever the issue affecting your teenager, talk about it privately with your partner before broaching the subject with your child. Your private opinions may differ and that is bound to cause more trouble. Agree on whatever line you are going to take and then put it to the child as diplomatically as possible.

Voice your worries
If you are worried about your teenager's behaviour, don't keep it to yourself. Tell your partner and talk through the best course of action.

Talk to your teenager
Communication should never be reduced to a series of shouting matches, so keep your temper and offer a sympathetic ear whenever possible. Educate your children on the dangers of drugs, alcohol and underage sex, and make sure they know you are both available to talk should they have a problem. You don't always need to talk to your child with your partner, but decide beforehand which of you is the most appropriate person to deal with each situation.

Give them some leeway
Teenagers may be children to you, but they hate being treated as such. Set a time for them to come home and find out where they are going, then let them get on with it. If they are given some slack and prove they are trustworthy, you know you can give them a little more next time.

EMPTY NEST

As your children get older, you will have more and more time to spend together until, eventually, the birds have flown and you are back to a unit of two – at least for the majority of the time. After years of hearing a houseful of voices, it will become very quiet on the home front, and that can be a tricky time for any relationship.

Turn back time
Now is the moment to remember the strengths of your relationship and what drew you to each other in the first place. What did you both enjoy doing before the children came along?

What have you always wanted to try? Sit down over dinner and discuss the shared interests that you now have time to pursue. Perhaps you could join a dance class, take up photography or simply plan long walks in the country?

Lead separate lives

Few marriages benefit from your being in each other's pockets day in, day out. As well as having shared hobbies, it is a good idea to have interests away from your husband's, which will also widen your circle of friends. College courses, such as computing or cookery, are widely available, or you could join a club or voluntary organization in your local community.

Consider his feelings

He might not show it, but he will be missing the kids just as much as you are. When they call from university or from their new flat, make sure they speak to their dad as well – and not just to ask for money! Equally, if they are planning to pop round and see you, and it's a rare occurrence, ask them to come when he's at home too.

MODERN MARRIAGE

In the first year of marriage, the man speaks
and the woman listens.
In the second year, the woman speaks
and the man listens.
In the third year, they both speak
and the neighbours listen.

Tips for a
Happy Marriage

The following tips have been compiled by Relate, the UK's leading relationship support agency.

ACCEPT DIFFERENCE

We are all unique individuals and therefore differences of opinion and personality are normal. Couples will argue – accept it as an everyday part of healthy family life.

EXPLORE
AND LEARN TOGETHER

Couples can grow together by learning new things together. Taking up a new activity where you're both novices can be a very bonding experience.

TOUCH REGULARLY

Human touch has the power to soothe, support and encourage, whether it's a peck on the cheek, a hug or making love.

LAUGH TOGETHER

Take time to sit down together and watch a comedy or play a game that will make you laugh. Laughter releases endorphins, which are nature's feel-good chemicals, and when you laugh together you create a positive atmosphere.

MAKE TIME TO BE ALONE

Everyone needs time and space to themselves – some need a lot, others just a little. Accept that you're different and give each other space so you can more fully enjoy the time you spend together.

'For marriage to be a success, every woman and every man should have their own bathroom!'

CATHERINE ZETA-JONES

SHARE GOALS

Another way to connect emotionally is to talk about, and work towards, common goals. It doesn't matter if it's tidying up the garage, landscaping the garden or climbing a mountain, the important thing is that it's shared.

TREAT OTHERS AS YOU WISH TO BE TREATED

If you want to be treated with respect, then respect each other. If you want others to be kind and courteous, then be kind and courteous yourself.

SPEND TIME WITH OTHER COUPLES

It's easy to think that only you have problems, but when you spend time with other couples you'll see that you're not alone. In fact, you may come home appreciating the strength of your relationship.

ACCEPT YOUR MISTAKES AND SAY SORRY

Love does not mean never having to say you're sorry. We all make mistakes and get it wrong sometimes. It takes practice to be a partner, and admitting your mistakes will encourage others to do likewise.

GIVE EACH OTHER THE BENEFIT OF THE DOUBT

Don't jump to conclusions. If you feel irritated about something, first check that what you think they're saying is what they mean. If it wasn't, then let it go; if it was, sit down calmly and discuss the problem.

'The problem with marriage is that it ends
every night after making love, and it must be rebuilt
every morning before breakfast.'
GABRIEL GARCÍA MÁRQUEZ

Anecdotes

FAUX PAS

Former First Lady Barbara Bush was on a state visit to Japan with her husband, George, when they attended a formal luncheon at the Imperial Palace in Tokyo. At the meal she was seated next to Japan's Emperor Hirohito, with whom she struck up a conversation about the relatively new building.

'Was the former palace so old that it crumbled?' she asked innocently.

'No,' Hirohito shot back. 'I'm afraid that you bombed it . . .'

HANKS A LOT, TOM

Natalie Moore's wedding-day nerves were sent sky high when she was held up by road closures in Rome that threatened to make her late for her nuptials. In fact, it was the filming of the upcoming movie *Angels and Demons* that was causing the hold-up. Her worries turned to shock when Oscar-winning actor Tom Hanks halted filming and rushed off the set to personally escort her through the closed streets to the ceremony.

It certainly was a *Big* day for Natalie!

FEELING A BIT CROC

A romantic wedding in Mexico ended in disaster for one guest after he was attacked by a crocodile.

Irishman Sean Treacy was at the wedding reception in Cancún when he was bet $20 to swim in the Nichupte Lagoon. He dived straight into the waiting jaws of a crocodile, who took a bite out of his arm.

No doubt that wasn't the sort of wedding snap he had in mind.

FREUDIAN SLIP

As French President Charles de Gaulle neared retirement, his wife, Yvonne, was asked by Harold Macmillan's wife, Dorothy, what she most looked forward to in the coming years.

'A penis,' she announced, rendering the assembled company speechless.

After a few moments of embarrassed silence her husband came to the rescue.

'My dear,' he told her, 'I think the English don't pronounce the word quite like that. It's 'appiness!'

DOTING HUSBANDS

Hard work is the cornerstone of Japanese society, and many men work such long hours that they see very little of their wives. To counteract this trend, a group of loving husbands has banded together to form Nihon Aisaika Kyokai or Japan Doting Husbands Association.

Businessman Kiyotaka Yamana came up with the idea after his wife divorced him for not taking her seriously and not spending time with her. When he remarried, he vowed not to make the same mistake again and set up the association to encourage other men to do the same.

He designated 31 January 'Beloved Wives Day', when men should return home early from work and shower their spouses with love and attention, and set out the following rules:

THE GOLDEN RULES
OF DOTING HUSBANDS

* Get home by 8 p.m.

* Eat dinner with your family

* Say thanks to your wife for all that she does

* Call your wife by name rather than saying 'you' or grunting at her

* Look your wife in the eyes when your talk to her

MAN-EATER

Zsa Zsa Gabor was once asked how many husbands she'd had. 'You mean, apart from my own?' she quipped.

On another occasion, a women's magazine asked a selection of famous women what they first noticed about a woman.

'Her way of speaking,' said Agatha Christie.

'Her hands,' said Maria Callas.

'Her husband,' said Zsa Zsa.

SUPERMAN

Six-times-married Hedy Lamarr once commented, 'I must quit marrying men who feel inferior to me. Somewhere there must be a man who could be my husband and not feel inferior. I need a superior inferior man.'

DOMESTIC DISASTER

As a young bride, Hilary returned from her honeymoon full of plans to become the perfect wife. Having waved her husband off to work on her first day in their new home, she hung the second load of washing out on her new washing line, then resolved to make him something special for dinner.

In her brand-new soufflé dish – a wedding present from a relative – she lovingly prepared a soufflé and proudly popped it in the oven.

Just before her husband returned, she looked out the window to see that the washing line had broken and deposited the entire load in the mud. When she checked on the soufflé, the dish had split in two and the entire contents were a sludgy mess on the bottom of the oven.

The omens had been there on her wedding day when Hilary walked up the aisle with a burn mark on her face after being told that you could tell if a sponge cake was cooked by listening to it!

> 'The people people have for friends
> Your common sense appall
> But the people people marry
> Are the queerest folk of all.'
>
> **CHARLOTTE PERKINS GILMAN**

MEET THE IN-LAWS

After she had been dating Jim for a few months, Ali overindulged on wine during a night out together. After dinner, the couple had a blazing row and a furious Ali said that was it, the relationship was over, before storming out of the restaurant.

She made it to the Underground, got on the tube and promptly fell asleep. The next thing she knew she was in an unknown part of West London, seriously tipsy, having missed her last train home.

As the only person she knew in London was her recently dumped boyfriend, she rang him and was horrified when his dad offered to come and pick her up. Jim's parents, whom she had never met before, then drove halfway across London in the middle of the night to pick her up and take her home.

Luckily the couple got back together and eventually married, but what a way to meet your future in-laws!

WEDDING WHEELS

A Chinese couple who got hitched in June 2008 made their ceremony 'wheely' special by arriving on rollerblades and insisting that all the wedding guests do the same. After the vows, in Heilongjiang, China, the whole wedding party whizzed down the road to the reception, accompanied by traffic cops.

NAKED CHEF

Celebrity chef Jamie Oliver once planned a naughty surprise for his wife, Jools, on Valentine's Day. He stripped off his clothes while cooking a special roast dinner, but burned his wedding tackle on the oven door. 'I really ruined my evening,' he said later. 'And my night!'

'Husbands are like fires.
They go out when unattended.'

ZSA ZSA GABOR

Jokes About Wives

MARRIED LIFE

Three women, one a girlfriend, one a mistress and one married, decided to surprise their men by dressing up in sexy leather outfits, high heels and leather masks. A few days later they compared notes: 'My boyfriend came home and found me in the leather bodice, stilettos and mask,' said the girlfriend. 'He was so thrilled he said, "You are the woman for me. Will you marry me?" Then we made love all night long.'

'I met my man at our little love-nest,' said the mistress. 'I was in the leather bodice, stilettos and mask and he was speechless, but we had great sex all night.'

'I sent the kids to my mother's for the night,' said the wife. 'Then I put on the leather bodice, stilettos and mask. My husband came home from work, opened the door and said, "All right, Batman, what's for dinner?"'

'Before marriage, a girl has to make love to a man to hold him. After marriage, she has to hold him to make love to him.'

MARILYN MONROE

TILL DEATH US DO PART

An ageing couple were afraid there might be no life after death, so they made a pact that whoever went first would return with news of what lies beyond. The husband was the first to go, and shortly after his funeral, his spirit paid a visit.

'Is that you, Harry?' said his wife.

'Yes, I've come back, like we agreed,' he replied.

'What's it like?' she asked.

'Well, I get up in the morning and I have sex. Then I have breakfast, go off to the golf course and have sex; I sunbathe and then I have sex twice. Then I have lunch, go round the golf course again, then have sex for the rest of the afternoon. After supper it's back to the golf course, then I have sex until late at night. The next day I do it all over again.'

'Oh, Harry, you really are in heaven,' said his astounded wife.

'Not exactly,' replied Harry. 'I'm a rabbit in Surrey.'

'I've often wanted to drown my troubles,
but I can't get my wife to go swimming.'

PETER KAY

FROG STORY

A woman was walking through the woods one day when she met a frog that had its foot trapped. 'Please release me,' said the frog, 'and I will grant you three wishes.' The lady did as he asked and the frog thanked her, but added, 'I forgot to tell you that there is a condition to your wishes. Whatever you wish for yourself, your husband will get ten times over.'

First she wished to be the most beautiful woman in the world.

'You do realize that this wish will also make your husband the most handsome man in the world, so women will find him irresistible,' warned the frog.

'But I will be the most beautiful woman so he will have eyes only for me,' she argued.

With a flick of his tongue, the frog turned her into the most beautiful woman in the world. Next she wished to be the richest woman in the world, and again the frog warned that her husband would be ten times richer. 'But what's mine is his and what's his is mine,' she reasoned.

With a flick of his tongue, the frog turned her into the richest woman in the world.

'You have one wish left,' he said. 'What will it be?'

Without hesitation she replied: 'I'd like a mild heart attack!'

MORAL MAZE

Two vicars were discussing the decline in moral standards in modern-day society.

'I didn't sleep with my wife before we were married,' said one clergyman piously. 'Did you?'

'I don't know,' said the other. 'What was her maiden name?'

'I should like to see any kind of a man, distinguishable from a gorilla, that some good and even pretty woman could not shape a husband out of.'

**OLIVER WENDELL HOLMES SENIOR,
WRITER AND PHYSICIAN**

'Do not marry a man to reform him.
That is what reform schools are for.'

MAE WEST

WHAT'S MINE IS YOURS

An elderly couple in a burger restaurant ordered one meal and an extra cup. Then the old man carefully divided the burger and shared out the fries one by one before pouring half the soft drink into the other cup. Then he began to eat, while his wife sat quietly with her hands in her lap.

A member of staff who'd been watching intently asked why they didn't get a meal each.

'We've been married fifty years and everything has, and always will be, shared fifty-fifty,' explained the old lady.

Then the young man asked the wife why she wasn't eating her half of the meal and she replied, 'It's his turn to use the teeth.'

COP THAT

A policeman in a small town pulled over a speeding motorist.

'But, officer,' the young man said, 'I can explain.'

'Be quiet,' snapped the officer. 'You can cool down in jail until the chief gets back.'

'But, officer–' the man began.

'I said to keep quiet,' interrupted the policeman as he threw him in jail.

A few hours later the policeman popped his head around the cell door and said, 'The chief will be here soon. It's lucky for you he's been at his daughter's wedding so he'll be in a good mood.'

'I doubt it,' retorted the young man. 'I'm the groom.'

DINING OUT

As John and Julia celebrated their thirtieth wedding anniversary, many people asked them the secret of a long marriage.

'Simple,' said Julia. 'We take time to go to a restaurant twice a week for a candlelit dinner, a relaxing glass of wine, some soft music, and a slow walk home.'

'Yes,' agreed John. 'She goes on Wednesdays and I go on Fridays!'

SECRET LOVE

After many, many years of marriage, Tom and Joan knew everything about each other. They had shared everything. They had talked about everything. There was only one secret between them. Joan kept a locked box under the bed that she had warned her husband never to open.

Tom rarely thought about the box, or its contents, until Joan became gravely ill and was told she had little time left. Finally, Tom asked his ailing wife what she hid inside the box. She agreed that it was time he should know, and so she gave him the key.

Inside, he found two knitted toys and a stack of money, which came to nearly £100,000. Mystified, he asked Joan to explain.

'When we got married,' she told him, 'my mother told me that the secret of a happy marriage was to avoid argument. If I got angry, I should take myself elsewhere and knit something, so that's why I made the toys.'

Proudly, old Tom observed that there were only two toys, meaning she had only been angry twice in all their years of marriage.

'That explains the toys,' he said. 'What about the money?'

'Oh, that,' she replied. 'It's the money I made from selling the other toys.'

The Cooks' Book
For The Cook Who's Best At Ev...
ISBN 978-1-84317-328-1   Price: £9...

The Gardeners' Book:
For The Gardener Who's Best At Everything
ISBN 978-1-84317-327-4   Price: £9.99

The Family Book:
Amazing Things To Do Together
ISBN: 978-1-906082-10-9   Price £14.99

The Christmas Book:
How To Have The Best Christmas Ever
ISBN: 978-1-84317-282-6   Price: £9.99

These titles and all other Michael O'Mara Books
are available by post from:
Bookpost Ltd
PO Box 29, Douglas, Isle of Man IM99 1BQ

To pay by credit card, use the following contact details:

Telephone: **01624 677237** / Fax: **01624 670923**
Email: **bookshop@enterprise.net**
Internet: **www.bookpost.co.uk**

Postage and packing is free in the UK;
overseas customers should allow £5 per hardback book.